Extended

Mathematics

for IGCSE®

Revision
Guide

June Haighton
Andrew Manning
Gina McManus
Margaret Thornton
Keith White

Series Editor:
Paul Metcalf

Nelson Thornes

Published in 2012 by:
Nelson Thornes Ltd
Delta Place
27 Bath Road
CHELTENHAM
GL53 7TH
United Kingdom

12 13 14 15 16/ 10 9 8 7 6 5 4 3 2 1

A catalogue record for this book is available from the British Library

ISBN 978 1 4085 1653 9

Cover photograph: Franck Boston/iStockphoto
Page make-up and illustrations by Tech-Set Ltd, Gateshead
Printed in China

This resource has not been through the Cambridge endorsement process.

Contents

Introduction

This book has been written to support *Extended Mathematics for Cambridge IGCSE*. It has been collated by teachers and examiners to help you revise for your IGCSE exam. The authors have worked together to ensure that the content reflects the IGCSE syllabus and highlights the essential features of each topic area.

Each chapter has the following features to make learning as interesting and effective as possible:

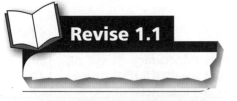

Learning outcomes

After this chapter you should be able to:
● factorise expressions [C]

The **learning outcomes** at the start of the chapter give you an idea of the content of the chapter. They also offer you a graded checklist so you can assess what you know and understand.

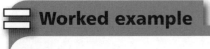

Revise 1.1

Revise: Each chapter is divided into a series of Revise sections to carefully take you through the required content. The Revise sections include key information which you should know for your exam.

Worked example

Worked example: Each Revise includes a worked example or examples to illustrate and extend the content. You should work through the worked examples yourself and compare your answers with the solutions given.

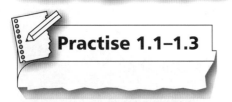

Practise 1.1–1.3

Practise: Each Revise section is followed by a Practise section which includes questions that allow you to practise what you have just revised. The questions are carefully chosen to mirror the style of the exam papers.

Exam tip

Exam tip: Regular exam tips are included to help you avoid common errors and mistakes. Make sure you read these tips very carefully as they will help you a lot in your exam.

Practice exam questions

Practice exam questions appear at the end of the book. These offer further practice for your exams. You should work through the exam questions when you have completed the book.

Key words: The first time they appear in this book key words are highlighted in **bold** text. A definition can be found in the glossary section at the back of the book so that you can check the meaning of words and practise your mathematics vocabulary.

1 Angles

Revise 1.1 Geometry

Angles

A full turn is 360° (**degrees**).

The **angle** between **perpendicular lines** is a **right angle**. This is 90° (a quarter turn).

An **acute** angle is less than 90°. An **obtuse** angle is greater than 90°, but less than 180°.

A **reflex** angle is greater than 180°, but less than 360°.

Angles at a point add up to 360°.	**Angles on a straight line add up to 180°.**	**Vertically opposite angles are equal.**

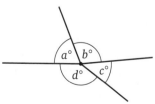

$a + b + c + d = 360$

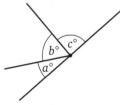

$a + b + c = 180$

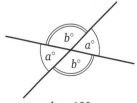

$b = 180 - a$

Parallel lines

Alternate angles **are equal.**	**Corresponding angles** **are equal.**	**Interior angles** add up to 180°.
$a = c$ and $b = d$	$a = e, b = f, c = g,$ and $d = h$	$a + d = 180$ and $b + c = 180$

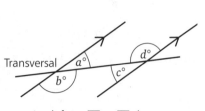

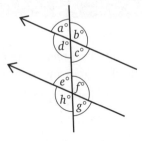

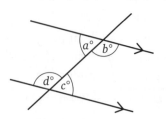

Look for a $\diagup$ or $\diagdown$ shape	Look for a $\sqsubset$ or $\sqsupset$ shape	Look for a $\sqsubset$ or $\sqsupset$ shape

Triangles and quadrilaterals

The angle sum of a triangle = 180°. The angle sum of a quadrilateral = 360°.

Special triangles and quadrilaterals

The properties that you should know are shown below.

Equilateral triangle	**Isosceles triangle**	**Scalene triangle**
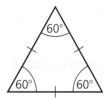	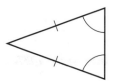	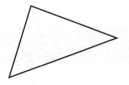
All sides equal Each angle is 60°	Two equal sides Two equal angles	All sides different All angles different

Square	**Rectangle**	**Rhombus**
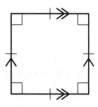	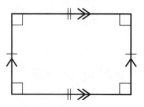	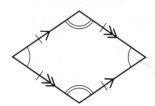
All sides equal Opposite sides parallel Each angle is 90°	Opposite sides equal Opposite sides parallel Each angle is 90°	All sides equal Opposite sides parallel Opposite angles equal

Parallelogram	Trapezium	Kite
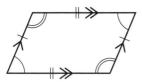	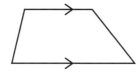	
Opposite sides equal Opposite sides parallel Opposite angles equal	One pair of parallel sides (In an isosceles trapezium the non-parallel sides are equal)	Two pairs of adjacent sides equal One pair of equal angles

You also need to know about the symmetries of these shapes (see Revise 9.1).

Congruence and similarity

Congruent shapes are exactly the same shape and size. They have equal angles and equal sides. Each of the following tests is enough to prove that two triangles are congruent:

- the 3 sides of one triangle are equal to the 3 sides of the other triangle (which can be written as **SSS**)
- 2 sides and the angle between them in one triangle are equal to 2 sides and the angle between them in the other triangle (which can be written as **SAS**)
- 2 angles and a side in one triangle are equal to 2 angles and the corresponding side in the other triangle (which can be written as **AAS**)
- both triangles are right-angled and the hypotenuse and one other side are equal (which can be written as **RHS**).

Similar shapes are the same shape, but different in size. They have equal angles and corresponding sides are in the same ratio.

If corresponding lengths in the two similar shapes are in the ratio $a : b$

- corresponding areas are in the ratio $a^2 : b^2$
- corresponding volumes are in the ratio $a^3 : b^3$.

Worked examples

Triangles and quadrilaterals

D E

Find the values of a and b. Give reasons for your answers.

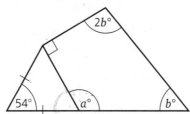

Solution

The triangle is isosceles with equal angles $= \dfrac{180° - 54°}{2} = 63°$ ◄── | Angle sum of a triangle = 180°. |

$a = 180 - 63 = 117$ ◄─────────────────── | Angles on a straight line add up to 180°. |

$b + 2b + 90 + 117 = 360$ ◄──────── | Angle sum of a quadrilateral = 360°. |

$$3b = 360 - 207$$
$$b = 153 \div 3$$
$$b = 51$$

Parallel lines and similar triangles   C B

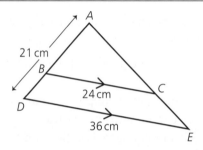

a In the diagram $AD = 21$ cm, $DE = 36$ cm and $BC = 24$ cm. Calculate the length of BD.

b The area of triangle ADE is 216 cm². Calculate the area of trapezium $BCED$.

Solution

a Angle ADE = angle ABC ◄────── | Corresponding angles are equal since BC is parallel to DE. |

Angle DAE = angle BAC ◄────────── | Since these are the same angle. |

Angle AED = angle ACB ◄────── | Corresponding angles are equal since BC is parallel to DE. |

So triangles $\dfrac{ABC}{ADE}$ are similar and corresponding sides are in the same ratio.

$\dfrac{AB}{AD} = \dfrac{BC}{DE}$ gives $\dfrac{AB}{21} = \dfrac{24}{36}$ ◄── | Putting the unknown side as the numerator makes the working easier. |

Cancelling gives $\dfrac{AB}{21} = \dfrac{2}{3}$

so $AB = \dfrac{2 \times 21}{3} = 14$ cm

$BD = AD - AB = 21 - 14 = 7$ cm

b Lengths in triangles ABC and ADE are in the ratio $2 : 3$, so areas are in the ratio $2^2 : 3^2 = 4 : 9$

$\dfrac{\text{Area of triangle } ABC}{\text{Area of triangle } ADE} = \dfrac{4}{9}$ so $\dfrac{\text{Area of triangle } ABC}{216} = \dfrac{4}{9}$

Area of triangle $ABC = \dfrac{4}{9} \times 216 = 96$ cm²

Area of trapezium $BCED$ = Area of triangle ADE − Area of triangle ABC

$$= 216 - 96 = 120 \text{ cm}^2$$

Revise 1.2 Angle properties

Angle sums of polygons

Any **polygon** can be split into triangles.

For example, a pentagon has 5 sides. It can be split into 3 triangles.

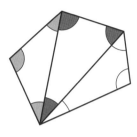

So the angle sum of a pentagon = 3 × 180°

The number of triangles is two less than the number of sides.

Angle sum of any polygon = (number of sides − 2) × 180°.

A **regular** polygon has all sides equal and all angles equal.

The table gives the angles of some regular polygons.

Name of polygon	Number of sides	Number of triangles	Sum of interior angles	When the polygon is regular, each angle =
Triangle	3	1	1 × 180° = 180°	180° ÷ 3 = 60°
Quadrilateral	4	2	2 × 180° = 360°	360° ÷ 4 = 90°
Pentagon	5	3	3 × 180° = 540°	540° ÷ 5 = 108°
Hexagon	6	4	4 × 180° = 720°	720° ÷ 6 = 120°
Heptagon	7	5	5 × 180° = 900°	900° ÷ 7 = $128\frac{4}{7}°$
Octagon	8	6	6 × 180° = 1080°	1080° ÷ 8 = 135°
Nonagon	9	7	7 × 180° = 1260°	1260° ÷ 9 = 140°
Decagon	10	8	8 × 180° = 1440°	1440° ÷ 10 = 144°

A regular triangle is equilateral.

A regular quadrilateral is a square.

The sum of the exterior angles of any polygon = 360°.

At each vertex of the polygon,
interior angle + exterior angle = 180°.

For example, each exterior angle of a
regular hexagon = 360° ÷ 6 = 60°
and each interior angle = 180° − 60° = 120°.

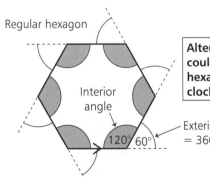

Regular hexagon

Interior angle

120° 60°

Alternatively you could go around the hexagon in a clockwise direction.

Exterior angle = 360° ÷ 6 = 60°

Exam tip

Using the sum of the exterior angles equals 360° is often the quickest way to solve problems involving polygons.

Worked example

Polygons

C

The diagram shows part of a regular polygon.

Each interior angle of the polygon is 144°.

What is the name of this polygon?

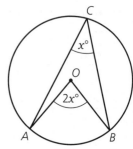

Solution

The exterior angle of this polygon $= 180° - 144° = 36°$. ◄

> Angles on a straight line add up to 180°.

The number of exterior angles $= 360° \div 36° = 10$. ◄

> Since the sum of the exterior angles of a polygon is 360°.

The polygon has 10 sides, so the polygon is a decagon.

Revise 1.3 Circle properties

Circle properties

The angle subtended by an **arc** (or **chord**) at the centre of a circle is twice the angle subtended at any point on the circumference.

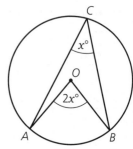

This means that the angle subtended at the circumference by a diameter is a right angle. In other words, the angle in a **semicircle** is always 90°.

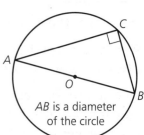

AB is a diameter of the circle

The angles subtended by the same arc (or chord) are equal.

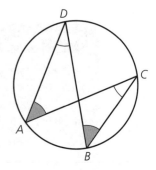

The opposite angles of a **cyclic quadrilateral** are supplementary (this means their sum is 180°).

$$p + r = 180$$
$$q + s = 180$$

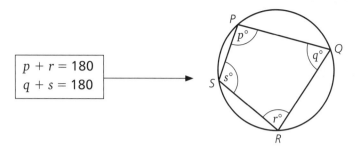

A **tangent** is always perpendicular to the radius drawn at the point where the tangent touches the circle.

Tangents from an external point are equal in length.

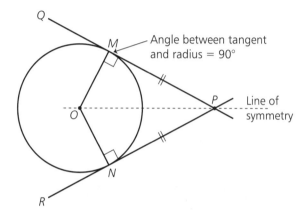

Angle between tangent and radius = 90°

Line of symmetry

The perpendicular from the centre to a chord bisects the chord.

The perpendicular *OM* cuts the chord *AB* in half.
AM = *MB*.

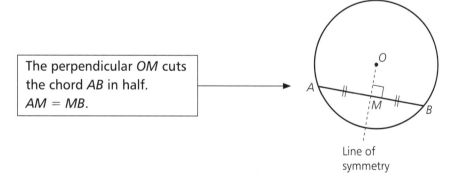

Line of symmetry

Equal chords are equidistant from the centre of the circle.

AB = *CD*
so *OM* = *ON*

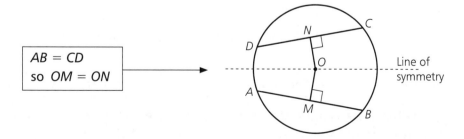

Line of symmetry

Worked examples

Circle chord properties

B

A circle, centre O and diameter 12 cm, has a chord AB of length 7.2 cm.

Find the distance from O to AB.

Solution

The diagram shows the circle and the chord AB.

OB = the radius of the circle = 12 cm $\div$ 2 = 6 cm.

M is the midpoint of the chord with MB = 7.2 cm $\div$ 2 = 3.6 cm.

Using Pythagoras in triangle OMB

$OM^2 = 6^2 - 3.6^2 = 36 - 12.96 = 23.04$

$OM = \sqrt{23.04} = 4.8$ cm

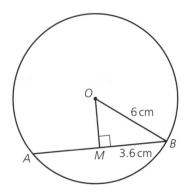

Circle angle properties

B

P, Q, R and S lie on a circle, centre O.
TPU and TSV are tangents to the circle.

Find the size of the angles marked by letters.

Give reasons for your answers.

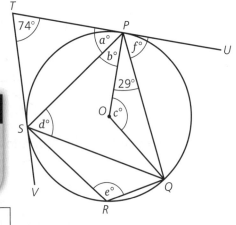

> **Exam tip**
>
> Remember that equal tangents and equal radii of a circle often give useful isosceles triangles.
>
> **Note 'radii' is the plural of 'radius'.**

Solution

$a = \dfrac{180 - 74}{2} = 53$ ◄── *TP* and *TS* are equal tangents, so a° is one of the equal angles of isosceles triangle *TPS*.

$b = 90 - 53 = 37$ ◄── The angle between tangent *TP* and radius *OP* is 90°.

$c = 180 - 2 \times 29 = 122$ ◄── *OP* and *OQ* are radii, so triangle *OPQ* is isosceles with two angles of 29°.

$d = 122 \div 2 = 61$ ◄── Angle *POQ* at the centre is twice angle *PSQ*, the angle at the circumference on the same arc *PQ*.

$e = 180 - (b + 29)$ ◄── Opposite angles of cyclic quadrilateral *PQRS* add up to 180°.

$\quad = 180 - 66 = 114$

$f = 90 - 29 = 61$ ◄── The angle between tangent *PU* and radius *OP* is 90°.

> **Often there is more than one way to find an angle. Here f could be found by using the sum of the angles on line *TPU* (180 − 53 − 37 − 29 = 61).**

Practise 1.1 – 1.3

1 a *ABCD* is a parallelogram. Angle *ABC* = 112°.

Find the other angles of the parallelogram, giving reasons for your answers.

b *PQRS* is a quadrilateral. *PQ* = *PS* and *QR* = *SR*.

The diagonals *PR* and *QS* intersect at a point *T*.

i Draw a sketch of *PQRS* and write down its name.

ii Name an angle that is equal to angle *PQR*.

iii Name a triangle that is congruent to triangle *RST*.

[Grades D–C]

2 a **i** Work out the size of the interior angles of a regular polygon that has 20 sides.

ii Use a different method to check your answer to part **a i**.

b A regular polygon has interior angles of 156°. Find the number of sides of the polygon.

c A pentagon has two right angles. The other angles are equal to each other.

Work out the size of these angles.

[Grade C]

3 a Find the following angles. Give reasons for your answers.

i Angle *STR*   **iii** Angle *PRQ*

ii Angle *PQR*   **iv** Angle *RPQ*

b *PQ* = 25 cm, *QR* = 15 cm and *SR* = 6 cm.
Calculate the length of *TS*.

c The area of triangle *PQR* is 150 cm².
Find the area of triangle *TSR*.

[Grades E–B]

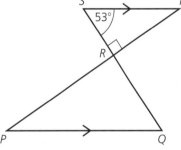

4 The radius of a circle is 6.5 cm long.

The distance from the centre of this circle to a chord is 2.5 cm.

Calculate the length of the chord.

[Grades C–B]

5 *A*, *B* and *C* lie on a circle, centre *O*, with diameter 20 cm.

AB = *BC* and the length of the tangent *CD* is 15 cm.

Calculate the length of: **a** *OD*   **b** *AB*.

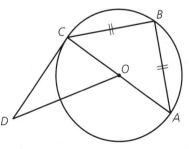

[Grade C]

6 Find each angle marked by a letter. Give a reason for each answer.

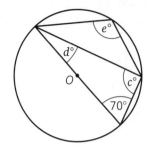 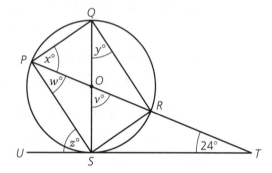 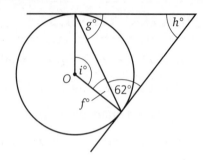

[Grade B]

7 Find each angle marked by a letter. Give a reason for each answer.

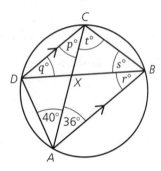 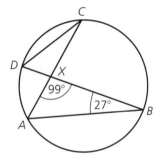

[Grade B]

8 *A* and *B* lie on a circle, centre *O*. *M* is the midpoint of chord *AB*.

Prove that triangles *OAM* and *OBM* are congruent.

[Grades B–A]

9 *A, B, C* and *D* lie on a circle. *AC* and *BD* intersect at *X*.

Angle *ABX* = 27° and angle *AXB* = 99°.

a Write down the size of angle *ACD*.

Give a reason for your answer.

b Find the size of angle *BDC*. Give reasons for your answer.

c Write down the geometrical word that completes the statement:

'Triangle *AXB* is …………….. to triangle *DXC*.'

d *AX* = 10.3 cm, *BX* = 18.6 cm and *CX* = 12.4 cm.

Calculate the length of *DX*.

e The area of triangle *ABX* is 94.6 cm².

Calculate the area of triangle *CDX*.

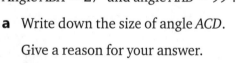
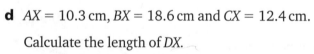

[Grades B–A]

10 a The interior angle of a regular polygon is 5 times as large as the exterior angle.
Calculate the number of sides of the polygon.

b *ABCDEFGH* is an octagon.
The interior angle *B* is 6° greater than the interior angle *A*.
The interior angle *C* is 6° greater than the interior angle *B*, and so on, with each of the next interior angles 6° greater than the previous one.
Calculate interior angle *A*.

[Grade B]

11 *A*, *B*, *C* and *D* lie on a circle, centre *O*.
SAT is the tangent at *A* and is parallel to *OB*.
Angle *TAB* = 47° and angle *COB* = 116°.

Calculate the size of angle *ADC*.

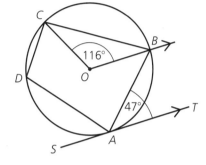

[Grade B]

12 Two similar bottles have heights that are in the ratio 3 : 4.

a The surface area of the larger bottle is 512 cm².

Calculate the surface area of the smaller bottle.

b The volume of the smaller bottle is 324 cm³.

Calculate the volume of the larger bottle.

[Grade A]

13 The surface area of a ball is 36π cm². The volume of this ball is 36π cm³.
The diameter of a larger ball is 50% greater than that of the first ball.
Calculate the surface area and volume of this larger ball.
Leave your answers in terms of π.

[Grade A]

Revise 2.1 Basic number

The structure of numbers

Natural numbers are the counting numbers 1, 2, 3, 4, 5, …

Natural numbers are given the symbol $\mathbb{N}$.

Integers are whole numbers …, $-5, -4, -3, -2 -1, 0, 1, 2, 3, 4, 5,$ …

Integers are given the symbol $\mathbb{Z}$.

Rational numbers are all the numbers that can be written in the form $\frac{p}{q}$, where p and q are integers. Integers, terminating decimals and recurring decimals are rational numbers.

Rational numbers are given the symbol $\mathbb{Q}$.

Irrational numbers are all the numbers that *cannot* be written in the form $\frac{p}{q}$.

The **real numbers** are all the rational numbers and irrational numbers.

Real numbers are given the symbol $\mathbb{R}$.

The **Venn diagram** shows the relationship between these numbers.

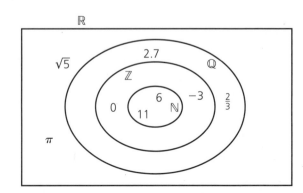

Ordering numbers

To order integers, draw or imagine a number line.

The numbers increase from left to right.

To order decimals, write them in a table with columns for each place value.

Put digits with the same place value in the same column.

Using the symbols =, ≠, <, >, ≤, ≥

- When two quantities are equal, you can show it with the equals sign, =.

- If quantities are not equal, you can use the 'is not equal to' sign, ≠.

- You could also write $\sqrt{15} < 4$, meaning '$\sqrt{15}$ is less than 4'.

- Also $\sqrt[3]{10} > 2$, $\sqrt[3]{10}$ is greater than 2.

- ≤ means 'is less than or equal to'.

- ≥ means 'is greater than or equal to'.

Types of number

Multiples, factors, primes and squares

A **multiple** is a number in the multiplication table of another number.

Multiples of 4 are 4, 8, 12, 16, 20, …

A **factor** is a number that divides exactly into another number with no remainder.

1, 2, 3, 4, 6 and 12 are factors of 12, because 12 can be divided exactly by 1, 2, 3, 4, 6, and 12.

A **prime number** is a number that has exactly two factors, 1 and itself.

2, 3 and 5 are prime numbers.

Square numbers are the result of multiplying an integer by itself.

Examples are 9 (= 3 × 3), 100 (= 10 × 10) and 25 (= 5 × 5).

Exam tip

- 1 is not a prime number as it has only one factor.
- 2 is the only even prime number.

Common multiples and common factors

A common multiple of two numbers is a number that is a multiple of both.

The **least common multiple (LCM)** of two numbers is the smallest number that is a multiple of both.

A common factor of two numbers is a number that is a factor of both.

The **highest common factor (HCF)** of two numbers is the largest number that is a factor of both.

Worked examples

Ordering numbers

E

Write these in order, starting with the smallest:

$\sqrt{10}$ $3\frac{1}{7}$ π 3.15

Solution

Write these numbers as decimals:

$\sqrt{10} = 3.1622 \ldots$ $3\frac{1}{7} = 3.1428 \ldots$ $\pi = 3.1415 \ldots$ $3.15 = 3.15$

Order the decimals:

$3.1415 \ldots$ $3.1428 \ldots$ 3.15 $3.1622 \ldots$

Then order the numbers in the original form:

π $3\frac{1}{7}$ 3.15 $\sqrt{10}$

Factors, multiples, primes and squares

C

Markus says that all numbers have an even number of factors.

Monika says that no prime numbers are square numbers.

Moshe says that the least common multiple of 56 and 42 is 336.

Only one person is correct. Who is correct?

Show that the other two are wrong.

Solution

Markus is wrong. All square numbers have an odd number of factors, e.g. the factors of 4 are 1, 2 and 4.

Monika is correct. A square number is made by multiplying a number by itself and so it cannot be prime.

Moshe is incorrect. 336 is a common multiple of 56 and 42, but 168 is the least common multiple.

Revise 2.2 Decimals, fractions and percentages

Working with decimals

To add or subtract decimals you must make sure that you line up the decimal points.

Put 0s in any spaces to avoid making mistakes.

You can multiply decimals using the grid method or the column method. Begin both methods by taking out the decimal point. When you have finished the calculation, use your rough estimate to put back in the decimal point.

Exam tip

When using a calculator, always do a rough estimate in your head. Make sure your answer is close to your rough estimate. If it isn't then you have made a mistake.

To divide decimals, rewrite the division so that you are always dividing by a whole number. Use equivalent fractions to do this.

For example, $24.72 \div 0.06 = \dfrac{24.72}{0.06}$

$$= \dfrac{2472}{6}$$ ← Multiply both numbers by 100.

$$= 2472 \div 6 = 412$$

Fractions

All fractions can be written in the form $\dfrac{a}{b}$.

$\dfrac{2}{3}$

The numerator is the number on the top of a fraction

The denominator is the number on the bottom

When fractions have different denominators, they are difficult to compare, so change them to **equivalent fractions**.

Equivalent fractions can be simplified by cancelling down or rewriting them in their **simplest form**.

This is done by dividing or multiplying both the numerator and the denominator by the same number. This is repeated until the fraction has the smallest possible whole number in its numerator and denominator.

Changing fractions to decimals

To change a fraction to a decimal, divide the numerator by the denominator.

Sometimes the division does not work out exactly, and you are left with a **recurring decimal**. Recurring decimals are shown by placing dots above a number or numbers that repeat.

For example, $0.\dot{6}$ is said as '6 recurring' and is a short way of writing $0.666666\ldots$

Also, $0.2\dot{1}41\dot{6}$ is a short way of writing $0.21416416416\ldots$

Changing decimals to fractions

To change a decimal to a fraction, you need to consider the place value of each digit.

Thousands	Hundreds	Tens	Units	.	Tenths	Hundredths	Thousandths
1000	100	10	1	.	0.1 or $\frac{1}{10}$	0.01 or $\frac{1}{100}$	0.001 or $\frac{1}{1000}$

A method for changing a recurring decimal to a fraction is shown in the second worked example. This involves multiplying the decimal by an appropriate multiple of 10 and subtracting so the recurring part is removed.

Changing percentages to fractions and decimals

One per cent (1%) means '1 out of every 100'.

A percentage is a number of hundredths.

To change a percentage to a fraction (or decimal), divide by 100.

To change a fraction or a decimal to a percentage

To change a fraction (or decimal) to a percentage, multiply by 100.

You can use what you know about equivalent fractions to rewrite a fraction with a denominator of 100.

Working with fractions

Addition and subtraction

You can add and subtract fractions only when their denominators are the same.

If the denominators are different, then you need to change them all to have the same denominator. If this is the smallest possible number then it is called the **lowest common denominator**.

Exam tip

Multiplying the denominators together will always give a common denominator, but it will not always be the lowest one.

Your calculations may involve **mixed numbers**.

Mixed numbers are fractions that consist of two parts: a whole number part and a fractional part.

Whole number part

$$2\frac{1}{3}$$ ← Fractional part

When you add or subtract mixed numbers, you deal with the whole numbers and the fractions separately.

Improper fractions are fractions where the numerator is larger than the denominator. If you obtain an improper fraction as an answer, change it to a mixed number.

Multiplication and division

To multiply fractions, begin by converting any mixed numbers to improper fractions. Then cancel down if possible. Next, multiply the numerators together and the denominators together. If the answer is an improper fraction, change it to a mixed number.

To multiply a fraction by an integer, write the integer as a fraction over 1, e.g. $7 = \frac{7}{1}$

To divide by a fraction you must *multiply* by the **reciprocal** of the fraction that follows the division sign. Change the ÷ sign to the × sign.

You find a reciprocal of a fraction by turning it upside down.

Ordering operations

Use **BIDMAS** for calculations involving more than one operation.

B Brackets

I Indices (powers: squares, cubes, …)

D Division

M Multiplication

⎫ Do these together, working from left to right

A Addition

S Subtraction

⎫ Do these together, working from left to right

Worked examples

Working with fractions   B A

Find the values for c and d in the following calculations:

a $\dfrac{3c}{8} - \dfrac{5c}{24} = \dfrac{1}{3}$

b $\dfrac{7}{8} \div \dfrac{14}{d} = \dfrac{3}{4}$

Solution

a $\dfrac{3c}{8} - \dfrac{5c}{24} = \dfrac{1}{3}$ ⟵ The lowest common denominator is 24.

$\dfrac{9c}{24} - \dfrac{5c}{24} = \dfrac{1}{3}$

$\dfrac{{}^{1}\cancel{4}c}{\cancel{24}_{6}} = \dfrac{1}{3}$ ⟵ Simplify the first fraction.

$\dfrac{c}{6} = \dfrac{1}{3}$ ⟵ Multiply both sides by 6.

$c = \dfrac{6}{3} = 2$

b $\dfrac{7}{8} \div \dfrac{14}{d} = \dfrac{3}{4}$ ⟵ Multiply by the reciprocal of the second fraction.

$\dfrac{{}^{1}\cancel{7}}{8} \times \dfrac{d}{\cancel{14}_{2}} = \dfrac{3}{4}$ ⟵ Cancel by 7.

$\dfrac{1}{8} \times \dfrac{d}{2} = \dfrac{3}{4}$ ⟵ Multiply the numerators, multiply the denominators.

$\dfrac{d}{16} = \dfrac{3}{4}$ ⟵ Multiply both sides by 16.

$d = \dfrac{3}{4} \times 16$

$d = 12$

Recurring decimals

C B

Change the recurring decimal $0.\overset{..}{2}\overset{.}{4}$ to a fraction in its lowest terms.

Solution

Let $x = 0.242424 \ldots$

> The first two digits repeat, so multiply both sides of the equation by 100.

$$100x = 24.242424 \ldots$$

> The decimal parts line up underneath each other.

$$x = 0.242424 \ldots$$

$$99x = 24$$

> So on subtracting they will disappear.

So
$$x = \frac{24}{99} = \frac{8}{33}$$

Therefore $0.\overset{..}{2}\overset{.}{4} = \dfrac{8}{33}$

Revise 2.3 Ratio and proportion

Simplifying ratios

A **ratio** compares two or more quantities with each other. It is written using a colon, e.g. $2:3$.

The order of a ratio is important.

A **proportion** compares one quantity with the total amount and is written as a fraction, e.g. $\frac{4}{5}$.

Ratios can be simplified by multiplying or dividing each part of the ratio by the same amount. This means that they can be simplified in the same way as for fractions.

A ratio is in its **simplest form** when it contains the smallest possible whole numbers.

You may be asked to write ratios in the form $1:n$ or $n:1$. These are called **unitary ratios**. For these ratios, you may leave decimals or fractions in the answer.

Dividing quantities in a given ratio

Some money is to be shared between two sisters in the ratio $x:y$.

The money must be divided into $(x + y)$ parts.

One sister gets x parts and the other gets y parts.

Example 1: Share $30 in the ratio $5:7$.

Solution: Divide $30 into 12 parts, as $5 + 7 = 12$.

$$\$30 \div 12 = \$2.50$$

The amounts are $5 \times \$2.50 = \$12.50$ and $7 \times \$2.50 = \$17.50$

Check that both of these answers add up to the total amount: $\$12.50 + \$17.50 = \$30$

Example 2: A map has a scale of 1 : 50 000.

Two towns are 9 km apart.

How far apart are they on the map?

Solution: 9 km = 9000 m = 900 000 cm

This is 50 000 parts in the ratio.

So one part = 900 000 cm ÷ 50 000 = 90 cm ÷ 5 = 18 cm

So on the map, they are 18 cm apart.

> ### Exam tip
>
> If you are asked to divide an amount in a given ratio, you can check your answer using this method:
> - add together all the parts of your answer
> - the sum should be the total value given in the original question.

Using ratios

The unitary method

To use the **unitary method,** calculate the value of one single unit, and then multiply to get the required answer.

For example, to find the cost of 9 glasses if 5 glasses cost $4:

one glass costs $4 ÷ 5 = $0.80

9 glasses cost 9 × $0.80 = $7.20

Direct proportion is when one variable increases in proportion with another variable.

For example, if the number of items increases, then so does the cost.

Inverse proportion is when one variable increases as the other decreases.

For example, if the number of people completing a particular task increases, then the time it takes for them to complete the same task decreases.

The multiplier method

To use the multiplier method, you multiply the quantity by the fraction representing the ratio.

For example, the ratio 3 : 2 can be used to form two fractions $\frac{3}{2}$ and $\frac{2}{3}$.

If you multiply by $\frac{3}{2}$, you will be increasing in the ratio 3 : 2.

If you multiply by $\frac{2}{3}$, you will be decreasing in the ratio 2 : 3.

Compound measures

A compound measure is made up of two other measures.

Speed, in kilometres per hour, is a compound measure made up from a measure of length (kilometres) and a measure of time (hours).

Problems that include compound measures can be answered using a formula triangle.

Average speed $(km/h) = \dfrac{\text{distance (km)}}{\text{time (hours)}}$, or $S = \dfrac{D}{T}$

This can be written in a triangle:

To calculate a time, cover up the T:

$$\text{time} = \frac{D}{S}$$

To calculate a distance, cover up the D:

$$\text{distance} = S \times T$$

Another example is:

$$\text{density} = \frac{\text{mass}}{\text{volume}}$$

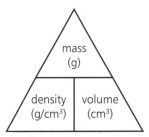

Always check that the units given in the question match each other. If not, change these before you start your calculations.

Direct and inverse proportion

y is **directly proportional to** x or $y \propto x$, if $y = kx$ (where k is a constant)

k is known as the **constant of proportionality**.

y is **inversely proportional to** x, or $y \propto \dfrac{1}{x}$, or $y = \dfrac{k}{x}$ (where k is a constant)

y can also be directly or inversely proportional to the squares, cubes, square roots, ... of x.

Worked examples

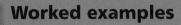

Dividing quantities in a given ratio D

A charity receives money from three different places: the government, local businesses and from collections at the local supermarket. This money is in the ratio $4:5:2$.

In one month, the total money received is $6160.

How much does the charity receive from the local supermarket collections?

Solution

Government : businesses : supermarket $= 4:5:2$

There are $4 + 5 + 2 = 11$ parts altogether.

$\frac{1}{11}$ of the money received $= \frac{1}{11} \times \$6160 = \$560$

So the money from the supermarket collections $= \frac{2}{11} \times \$6160 = 2 \times \$560 = \$1120$

You can check this answer. Work out all three different amounts and add them up. The total should be $6160.

Money from government $= \frac{4}{11} \times \$6160 = \$2240$

Money from businesses $\ \ = \frac{5}{11} \times \$6160 = \$2800$

Money from supermarket $= \frac{2}{11} \times \$6160 = \$1120$

Total $= \$2240 + \$2800 + \$1120 = \$6160$

Proportion B

If p varies inversely as q, and $p = 10$ when $q = 6$, find:

a p, when $q = 16$ **b** q, when $p = 1.5$

Solution

a $p \propto \dfrac{1}{q}$

   then

     $p = \dfrac{k}{q}$ where k is a constant.

   When $p = 10$, $q = 6$, so

     $10 = \dfrac{k}{6}$

     $60 = k$ ⟵ | Multiply both sides by 6. |

      $k = 60$

   The equation becomes

     $p = \dfrac{60}{q}$

   Substituting $q = 16$ into this equation gives:

     $p = \dfrac{60}{16}$

      $p = 3.75$

b Substituting $p = 1.5$ into the equation gives:

$$1.5 = \frac{60}{q}$$ ◄─────────────── Multiply both sides by q.

$$1.5q = 60$$ ◄─────────────── Divide both sides by 1.5.

$$q = \frac{60}{1.5}$$

$$q = 40$$

Practise 2.1 – 2.3

1 Calculate: $\dfrac{2.4 + 1.2^2 \times 40}{5^2 - 10 \div 2}$ [Grade D]

2 On a map, a length of 1 km is represented on the map by a length of 8 mm.

Find the ratio of the length on the map to the actual length in the form $1 : n$. [Grade D]

3 Find the least common multiple of 28 and 35. [Grade C]

4 Write these numbers in order of size, largest first.

28% $\frac{2}{7}$ 0.27 $\frac{3}{11}$ [Grade E]

5 $a \geqslant 6$ and $b < 2$.

Put a tick in a column to say whether these statements must be true, might be true or cannot be true.

	Must be true	Might be true	Cannot be true
$a > b$			
$a \div b = 3$			
$a + b > 4$			
$a - b > 4$			

[Grade C]

6 Write these numbers in the Venn diagram.

$\sqrt{10}$ $3\frac{1}{5}$ 4 -3

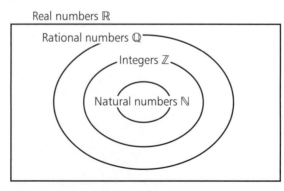

[Grade C]

7 Without finding the value of $\sqrt{15}$ or $\sqrt[3]{65}$, explain how you know that $\sqrt{15} < 4 < \sqrt[3]{65}$.

[Grade C]

8 Show that:

a $3\frac{3}{4} + 2\frac{3}{5} = 6\frac{7}{20}$

b $2\frac{5}{6} \div 1\frac{1}{3} = 2\frac{1}{8}$

Show all stages in your working. [Grade C]

9 A local farmer picks 5 boxes of oranges in 3 hours.

a How long would it take him to pick 4 boxes?

On another day, he picked 36 boxes of oranges in 10 hours.
The next day, he must pick another 36 boxes.
This time he has two friends to help him.

b How long will it take them?

Give your answers to both parts, **a** and **b**, in hours and minutes. [Grade C]

10 A man walked from his home to the next village, a distance of 15 km. It took him 2 hours and 45 minutes.

a Find his average speed in km/h.

Give your answer correct to 1 decimal place.

On the way back, he had to bring his father with him. The father could only walk at an average speed of 4.2 km/h.

b How long did it take them to return to the man's home?

Give your answer to the nearest minute. [Grade C]

11 There is a gap of T seconds between a person seeing a flash of lightning and hearing the thunder clap that follows. This time, T, is directly proportional to the distance, D kilometres, that the person is from the centre of the storm.

When the centre of the storm is 3 km away, the time gap is 9 seconds.

a When you are 7 km away, find the time gap between seeing the lightning and first hearing the thunder.

b How far away would you be if there was a time gap of 8 seconds? [Grade A]

3 Algebra

Revise 3.1 Basic algebra

Using letters for numbers

In algebra, a letter stands for an unknown number.

It is called a **variable** because it can take different values.

$4x + 2x + 5x − 3x$ is an **expression** and $4x$, $+2x$, $+5x$, $−3x$ are the **terms** of the expression.

To **simplify** the expression, add and subtract the number of x's.

$$4x + 2x + 5x − 3x = 8x$$

When the expression contains more than one variable, there will be **like terms** and **unlike terms**.

In the expression $2p + 4q − p + q − 2q$,

     $2p$ and $+4q$ are unlike terms,

     $2p$ and $−p$ are like terms and can be simplified to p, which you write as just p,

     $+ 4q + q − 2q$ are like terms and can be simplified to $+3q$.

       $2p + 4q − p + q − 2q = p + 3q$

> **Exam tip**
>
> The sign in front of each term 'belongs' to that term and stays with it when you collect like terms.

24

Expressing basic arithmetic processes algebraically

$3 \times a$ is written as $3a$. You do not show the multiplication sign.

$a \times b$ is written as ab.

This is the same as ba because 5×3 is the same as 3×5.

$a \times a$ is written as a^2.

$a \times a \times a$ is written as a^3.

In the expression $3a^2 + 2a - ab + 5a - a^2 + 4ba$,

$3a^2$ and $-a^2$ are like terms and can be simplified to $2a^2$

$+2a$ and $+5a$ are like terms and can be simplified to $+7a$

$-ab$ and $+4ba$ are like terms and can be simplified to $+3ab$

$$3a^2 + 2a - ab + 5a - a^2 + 4ba = 2a^2 + 7a + 3ab$$

Substitution

Replacing the letters in an expression with numbers to find its value is called **substitution**.

If you are given the expression $7x - 4y$, you can substitute numbers for x and y to find its value.

If $x = 5$ and $y = -2$, then $7x - 4y = (7 \times 5) - (4 \times -2)$

$$= 35 - (-8)$$
$$= 35 + 8$$
$$= 43$$

Using formulae

A **formula** can be written in words or in symbols.

The formula for the area of a triangle can be written as:

    Area equals half the base multiplied by the height.

Using A for the area, b for the base and h for the height, this can be written in symbols as:

    $A = \frac{1}{2}bh$

If you know the value of b and of h, you can then work out the area.

For example, if $b = 6.4 \text{ cm}$ and $h = 5 \text{ cm}$, then $A = \frac{1}{2} \times 6.4 \times 5 = 16 \text{ cm}^2$.

Worked example

Substitution   E

$x = 0.6$ and $y = -0.5$

Find the value of :

a $3x + 4y$ **b** $2x^2 - y^2$ **c** $\dfrac{5x}{4y}$

Solution

Start by writing down the expression, and then put in the numbers ($x = 0.6$, $y = -0.5$).

a $3x + 4y = (3 \times 0.6) + (4 \times -0.5)$

$\qquad = 1.8 + (-2)$

$\qquad = -0.2$

b $2x^2 - y^2 = (2 \times 0.6 \times 0.6) - (-0.5 \times -0.5)$

$\qquad = 0.72 - (0.25)$

$\qquad = 0.47$

c $\dfrac{5x}{4y} = \dfrac{5 \times 0.6}{4 \times -0.5}$

$\qquad = \dfrac{3}{-2}$

$\qquad = -1.5$

Revise 3.2 More algebra

Expanding brackets

To **expand** a bracket, you multiply each term inside the bracket by the term outside the bracket.

$\qquad 2p(p - 4) = 2p \times p + 2p \times -4$

$\qquad\qquad\quad = 2p^2 - 8p$

If an expression has more than one bracket, it may contain like terms.

$\qquad 2p(p - 4) + 5(p - 3) = 2p^2 - 8p + 5p - 15$

$\qquad\qquad\qquad\qquad\quad = 2p^2 - 3p - 15$

> **Exam tip**
>
> If an exam question says 'expand and simplify' there will be like terms to collect up.

Factorising expressions

To **factorise** an expression, you do the opposite of expanding a bracket.

You will be told to factorise an expression, such as $3q^2 + 2q$.

The two terms in this expression have a **common factor**, q.

$\qquad 3q^2 + 2q = q(3q + 2)$

> **Exam tip**
>
> After factorising, multiply out again to check your answer.

Constructing simple expressions

1 'Joe thinks of a number, doubles it and adds 9.'

Let the number be x.

This can be written in algebra as '$2x + 9$'.

2 'Jake is 2 years older than Paul and George is three times as old as Jake'.

Let Paul's age be *p* years.

Jake's age can be written as $(p + 2)$ years and George's age as $3(p + 2)$ years.

Exam tip

In the exam, you will probably be told which letter to use for the unknown number.

Solving linear equations

You will be asked to **solve** an equation to find the value of the **unknown** (for example, *x*).

You do this by reversing the operations, always doing the same to both sides of the equation.

1 In the equation $x - 6 = 2$, you add 6 to both sides to get $x = 8$.

2 In the equation $\frac{y}{5} = 3$, you multiply both sides by 5 to get $y = 15$.

If the equation has more than one operation, you have to think of the order of operations.

3 In the equation $8a + 1 = 25$, there are two operations: 'multiply *a* by 8 and then add 1'.

The second operation 'add 1' is the first one you reverse to solve the equation.

$$8a + 1 = 25$$

Subtract 1 from both sides: $8a = 24$

Divide both sides by 8: $a = 3$

4 You may have to find the equation first.

'Joe thinks of a number, doubles it and adds 9. His answer is 23.'

This can be written as the equation

$$2x + 9 = 23.$$

Exam tip

- It is usually a good idea to check your answer by substituting it back into the original equation.
- But if it is a very odd fraction such as $\frac{11}{17}$, (or a lengthy decimal) don't substitute!
- Instead, check your working as you have most probably made a mistake.

Changing the subject of a formula

The subject of a formula is the letter at the start of the formula, before the equals sign.

Changing the subject of (or **transforming**) the formula uses the same steps as for solving an equation.

The formula for the area of a triangle, $A = \frac{1}{2}bh$, can be transformed to become a formula to find the height.

Multiply both sides by 2: $2A = bh$

Divide both sides by *b*: $\frac{2A}{b} = h$

Write the answer in the form '$h = \ldots$' $h = \frac{2A}{b}$

Solving equations with the unknown on both sides

You have to collect all the terms in x (or whichever letter is used) on one side of the equation.

You have to collect all the other terms on the other side.

$$5x - 3 = 1 - 3x$$

This has $5x$ on the left and $-3x$ on the right.

$$5x - 3 + 3x = 1 - 3x + 3x$$

$$8x - 3 = 1$$

All the terms in x have been collected on the left.

$$8x - 3 + 3 = 1 + 3$$

$$8x = 4$$

All the other terms have been collected on the right.

$$x = \tfrac{1}{2}$$

Exam tip

Take great care with the signs in front of the terms.

Equations with brackets

Your first step is to remove the bracket, usually by multiplying it out.

Then solve the equation by doing the same to both sides.

For example, to solve the equation

$$4(y - 3) = 3y - 8$$

start by multiplying out $4(y - 3)$

$$4y - 12 = 3y - 8$$

then collect up terms to get

$$y = 4$$

Exam tip

Don't forget to multiply the second term in the bracket by the term in front of the bracket.

The worked example opposite shows how you can sometimes start by dividing both sides.

Equations with fractions

To solve an equation containing a fraction, you have to multiply both sides by the **denominator**.

Starting with $\qquad \dfrac{x}{3} = 12$

Multiply both sides by 3 $\quad x = 36$

If there is more than one fraction, multiply by the **lowest common denominator**.

Starting with $\qquad \dfrac{a}{4} = 10 - \dfrac{a}{6}$ $\qquad$ the lowest common denominator of 4 and 6 is 12.

Multiply both sides by 12 $\quad 12 \times \dfrac{a}{4} = 12 \times 10 - 12 \times \dfrac{a}{6}$

$$3a = 120 - 2a$$

$$5a = 120$$

$$a = 24$$

If there are two terms on top of the fraction, put brackets round them before you multiply, as shown in the worked example opposite.

Worked examples

Equations with brackets

D

Solve the equation $5(x - 2) = 30$

Solution

Multiply out the bracket $\quad 5x - 10 = 30$

Add 10 to both sides $\qquad\qquad 5x = 40$

Divide by 5 $\qquad\qquad\qquad x = 8$

Alternative solution

Divide both sides by 5 $\quad \dfrac{\overset{1}{\cancel{5}}(x - 2)}{\cancel{5}^1} = \dfrac{\overset{6}{\cancel{30}}}{\cancel{5}^1}$

$$x - 2 = 6$$

$$x = 8$$

Equations with fractions

B

Solve the equation $\quad \dfrac{2x + 5}{3} - \dfrac{6 - x}{2} = 1$

Solution

Put brackets round the terms on top of the fractions.

$$\frac{(2x + 5)}{3} - \frac{(6 - x)}{2} = 1$$

Multiply by the lowest common denominator, 6.

$$\overset{2}{\cancel{6}} \times \frac{(2x + 5)}{\cancel{3}^1} - \overset{3}{\cancel{6}} \times \frac{(6 - x)}{\cancel{2}^1} = 6 \times 1$$

$$2(2x + 5) - 3(6 - x) = 6$$

$$4x + 10 - 18 + 3x = 6 \qquad \boxed{-3 \times -x = +3x}$$

$$7x - 8 = 6$$

$$7x = 14$$

$$x = 2$$

Revise 3.3 Functions

Function notation

The function $f(x) = 11 - 2x$, tells us that the number, x, is multiplied by 2 and then subtracted from 11.

It may also be written as $f: x \rightarrow 11 - 2x$.

The equation $y = 11 - 2x$ describes the same operations.

For this function, $f(4) = 11 - 2 \times 4 = 3$ and
$$f(-1) = 11 - 2 \times -1 = 13$$

> **Exam tip**
>
> Remember BIDMAS when you substitute a value for x in the function.

Composite functions

$gf(x)$ is an example of a **composite function**.

$gf(x)$ means 'use function f first, followed by function g'.

If $f(x) = 6x$ and $g(x) = 2x + 9$

$$gf(-1) = g(-6)$$
$$= (2 \times -6) + 9 = -3$$

$gf(x)$ is not the same as $fg(x)$.

$$fg(-1) = f(2 \times -1 + 9)$$
$$= f(7) = 42$$

Inverse functions

$f^{-1}(x)$ is an inverse function.

$f^{-1}(x)$ is the function that reverses the processes of $f(x)$.

To find the inverse of a function, make x the subject of the formula.

To check your answer, use a number for x and find $f(x)$.

Then put the result number into the function $f^{-1}(x)$ and you should get back to your starting number.

Worked example

Functions

C B A

$f(x) = \dfrac{3x - 1}{2}$ and $g(x) = 4x$

a Find the value of x when $f(x) = 10$

b Express $fg(x)$ as a single function.

c Find $f^{-1}(x)$.

d Find the value of $gf^{-1}(10)$.

Solution

a $\dfrac{3x - 1}{2} = 10$

$3x - 1 = 20$

$3x = 21$

$x = 7$

b $fg(x) = f(4x)$

$= \dfrac{(3 \times 4x) - 1}{2}$

$= \dfrac{12x - 1}{2}$

c To find the inverse function, write f(x) as $y = \dfrac{3x - 1}{2}$

Make x the subject of the formula: $\qquad 2y = 3x - 1$

$2y + 1 = 3x$

$\dfrac{2y + 1}{3} = x$

The inverse function is $f^{-1}(x) = \dfrac{2x + 1}{3}$ ← | Remember to put x back in instead of y. |

d $f^{-1}(10) = \dfrac{2 \times 10 + 1}{3} = 7$

$gf^{-1}(10) = g(7)$

$= 28$

Practise 3.1 – 3.3

1 Simplify:

 a $x + 4y - 2y + 5x$

 b $2pq - p^2 + 5qp + 3p^2$

 c $m^3 - m - 3m + 5 - m^3$

[Grade E]

2 $a = -1$ and $b = -7$

 Find the value of: **a** $a^2 + b^2$ **b** $a^3 - b$.

[Grade D]

3 Use the formula $I = \dfrac{PRT}{100}$ to find I when $P = 2400$, $R = 2.25$ and $T = 3$.

[Grade D]

4 Multiply out and simplify $6(x - 1) - 2(3 + x)$.

[Grade C]

5 Factorise:

   a $12x + 4$ **b** $6uv - 2v$

[Grades D–C]

6 A melon costs $\$x$ and an orange costs $\$y$ dollars.

   Martina buys 4 melons and 15 oranges.

   Write down an expression in x and y for the total cost.

[Grade D]

7 Solve these equations.

   a $4p + 11 = 9$

   b $\dfrac{5q}{8} = 3$

   c $9 = 4(t - 1)$

[Grades E–D]

8 A taxi fare is worked out as a fixed charge of $12 plus $1.25 per kilometre.

   Roberto pays $20.75 for his journey of x kilometres.

   Write down an equation in x and solve it to find how far Roberto travelled.

[Grade C]

9 Make a the subject of the formula $P = 2a + 2b$

[Grade C]

10 Solve these equations.

   a $9x + 2 = 4(2x - 1)$

   b $\dfrac{2y + 7}{4} = 3$

   c $\dfrac{m + 3}{2} - \left(\dfrac{m - 3}{4}\right) = 4$

[Grades C–B]

11 $f(x) = x^2 + 1$ and $g(x) = 5 - x$

   a Find the value of $f(-6)$.

   b Show that $g^{-1}(x) = g(x)$.

   c Find $fg(4)$.

   d Express $gf(x)$ as a single function.

[Grades C–A]

Measures and mensuration

Learning outcomes

After this chapter you should be able to:

- use and convert units of mass, length, area, volume and capacity in practical problems `G F E D`
- carry out calculations involving perimeters and areas of rectangles, triangles, parallelograms and trapezia `F E D`
- carry out calculations involving the circumference and area of a circle `D`
- draw and recognise the nets of solids `G F E`
- carry out calculations involving the surface area of cuboids, cylinders, prisms and other solids `D C`
- carry out calculations involving the volume of cuboids, prisms and cylinders `E D C`
- calculate the length of an arc `B A`
- calculate the area of a sector `B A`
- calculate the surface area and volume of spheres, pyramids and cones from given formulae. `C B A`

Revise 4.1 Measures

You must know the metric units and **conversion factors** below.

To convert to a smaller unit, multiply by the conversion factor (so there are more of them).

To convert to a larger unit, divide by the conversion factor (so there are fewer of them).

Mass

1 tonne = 1000 kilograms (1 t = 1000 kg)

1 kilogram = 1000 grams (1 kg = 1000 g)

1 gram = 1000 milligrams (1 g = 1000 mg)

Length

1 kilometre = 1000 metres (1 km = 1000 m)

1 metre = 1000 millimetres (1 m = 1000 mm)

1 metre = 100 centimetres (1 m = 100 cm)

1 centimetre = 10 millimetres (1 cm = 10 mm)

> Remember kilo means 1000, milli means $\frac{1}{1000}$ and centi means $\frac{1}{100}$.

Capacity

1 litre = 1000 millilitres (1 l = 1000 ml)

1 litre = 100 centilitres (1 l = 100 cl)

1 centilitre = 10 millilitres (1 cl = 10 ml)

> Note also that 1 ml = 1 cm³ so 1 l = 1000 cm³ and 1 m³ = 1000 l.

Converting units of area and volume

Remember that the conversion factors for area and volume are not the same as those for length.

For example, $1\,m^2 = 100^2\,cm^2 = 10\,000\,cm^2$ and $1\,m^3 = 100^3\,cm^3 = 1\,000\,000\,cm^3$.

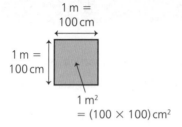

1 m =
100 cm

1 m =
100 cm

$1\,m^2$
$= (100 \times 100)\,cm^2$

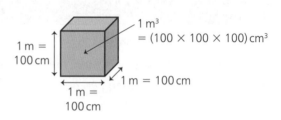

$1\,m^3$
$= (100 \times 100 \times 100)\,cm^3$

1 m =
100 cm

1 m = 100 cm

1 m =
100 cm

Worked example

Metric units
D C

The area of a lake on a map is $8\,cm^2$.

The actual area is 625 million times larger.

Find the actual area of the lake in km^2.

Solution

Actual area of lake $= 625\,000\,000 \times 8\,cm^2 = 5\,000\,000\,000\,cm^2$

$\qquad\qquad = 5\,000\,000\,000 \div 10\,000 = 500\,000\,m^2$

$\qquad\qquad = 500\,000 \div 1\,000\,000 = 0.5\,km^2$

$$1\,m^2 = 100^2\,cm^2 = 10\,000\,cm^2$$

$$1\,km^2 = 1000^2\,m^2 = 1\,000\,000\,m^2$$

> **Exam tip**
>
> To convert to a smaller unit, multiply by the conversion factor.
> To convert to a larger unit, divide by the conversion factor.

Revise 4.2 Mensuration: perimeter and area

Perimeter

The **perimeter of any shape is the total length of its sides.**

For example, the perimeter of a rectangle

$\qquad$ = length + width + length + width or 2(length + width).

In the metric system, perimeters are measured in mm, cm, m or km.

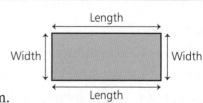

Length

Width

Width

Length

Area

Area is the amount of space inside a shape.

In the metric system, areas are measured in mm², cm², m² or km².

Area formulae

- Area of a rectangle = length × width

- Area of a parallelogram = base × perpendicular height

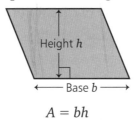

$$A = bh$$

- Area of a triangle = $\frac{1}{2}$ × base × perpendicular height

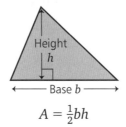

$$A = \tfrac{1}{2}bh$$

> Remember the height must be perpendicular to the base.

- Area of a trapezium

    = $\frac{1}{2}$ × sum of parallel sides × perpendicular height

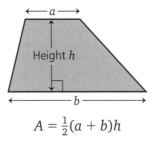

$$A = \tfrac{1}{2}(a + b)h$$

Circles

Length of the circumference of a circle, $C = \pi \times$ diameter $= \pi d = 2\pi r$.

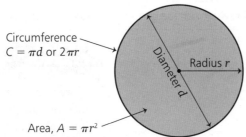

Circumference
$C = \pi d$ or $2\pi r$

Diameter d

Radius r

Area, $A = \pi r^2$

> The diameter is twice as long as the radius $d = 2r$.

Area of a circle, $A = \pi \times$ radius × radius $= \pi r^2$.

Worked examples

Perimeter and area of 2-D shapes

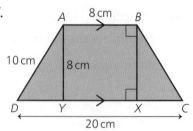

The diagram shows an isosceles trapezium *ABCD* and a square *ABXY*.

a Write the perimeter of *ABXY* as a fraction of the perimeter of *ABCD*, giving your answer in its simplest form.

b Write the area of *ABXY* as a percentage of the area of *ABCD*.

Solution

a Perimeter of *ABXY* = 32 cm

Perimeter of *ABCD* = 10 + 8 + 10 + 20 = 48 cm

Perimeter of *ABXY* as a fraction of the perimeter of *ABCD* = $\frac{32}{48} = \frac{2}{3}$ after cancelling

b Area of *ABXY* = 8 × 8 = 64 cm² ◄———— | *ABXY* is a square of side 8 cm.

Area of *ABCD* = $\frac{1}{2}$ × (8 + 20) × 8

$\qquad\qquad = \frac{1}{2}$ × 28 × 8

$\qquad\qquad = 112$ cm²

> **Area of a trapezium**
> = $\frac{1}{2}$ × **sum of parallel sides**
> × **perpendicular height**

> You can work this out by calculating 14 × 8 or 28 × 4 or $\frac{1}{2}$ of (28 × 8).

Area of *ABXY* as a percentage of the area of *ABCD* = $\frac{64}{112}$ × 100% = 57.1% (to 1 d.p.)

Composite shape

A triangular hole is cut from a circular card.

Calculate the area of the shaded part.

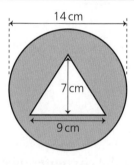

Solution

Area of circle = π × 7² = 153.9… cm² | **Area of circle = πr^2**

Area of triangle = $\frac{1}{2}$ × 9 × 7 | **Area of a triangle = $\frac{1}{2}$ × base × perpendicular height**

$\qquad\qquad = \frac{1}{2}$ × 63 = 31.5 cm²

Shaded area = 153.9… − 31.5

$\qquad\quad = 122.4… = 122$ cm² (to 3 s.f.)

> **Exam tip**
>
> Work as accurately as you can. Use the calculator's memory if necessary. Rounding values too soon may lose marks.

Revise 4.3 Mensuration: volume and surface area

Volume

Volume is the amount of space inside a 3-D shape.

In the metric system, volume is measured in mm^3, cm^3, m^3 or km^3.

Volume of a prism = area of cross-section × length

A cuboid and a cylinder are types of prism.

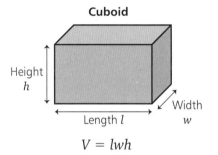

Cuboid

Height h
Length l
Width w

$$V = lwh$$

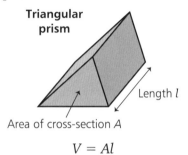

Triangular prism

Length l
Area of cross-section A

$$V = Al$$

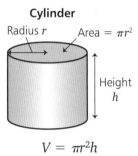

Cylinder

Radius r Area $= \pi r^2$
Height h

$$V = \pi r^2 h$$

Volume of a pyramid or cone $= \frac{1}{3}$ base area × perpendicular height

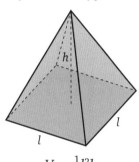

Square-based pyramid

h
l
l

$$V = \frac{1}{3}l^2h$$

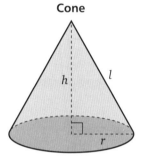

Cone

h l
r

$$V = \frac{1}{3}\pi r^2 h$$

> ### Exam tip
>
> Remember to put all dimensions into the same units before working out the area or volume of a shape.

Sphere

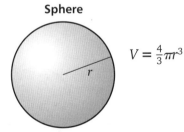

Volume of a sphere $= \frac{4}{3}\pi r^3$

r

$$V = \frac{4}{3}\pi r^3$$

The volume of a container is sometimes called its **capacity**.

Nets and surface area

A face is part of the surface of a solid – it is enclosed by edges.

An edge is a line where 2 faces meet.

A vertex is a point where 3 or more edges meet.

A cuboid has 6 **faces**, 12 **edges** and 8 **vertices**.

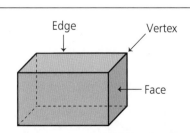

Edge   Vertex
Face

The **surface area** of a cube or cuboid is the total area of its 6 faces.

The diagram shows a **net** of the cuboid.

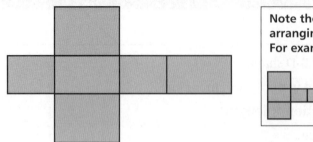

Note there are other ways of arranging the faces in the net. For example:

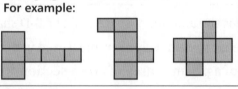

Surface area of a sphere, $A = 4\pi r^2$

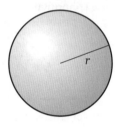

Curved surface area of a cone of radius r and sloping edge l is

$A = \pi r l$

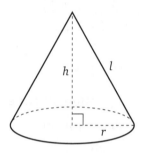

Worked examples

Net and surface area

C

A cylindrical can has diameter 7.6 cm and height 11.2 cm.

a Draw a sketch of the net of this can.

b Work out the total surface area of the can.

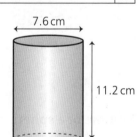

Solution

a The diagram shows the net of the can.

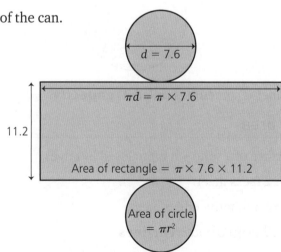

b The radius of each circle = 7.6 ÷ 2 = 3.8 cm

The area of each circle = $\pi r^2 = \pi \times 3.8 \times 3.8 = 45.364\ldots$ ← | Put this value into your calculator's memory to use later. |

The length of the rectangle = $\pi \times 7.6$

The area of the rectangle = $\pi \times 7.6 \times 11.2 = 267.412\ldots$

Total surface area of the cylinder = $267.412\ldots + 2 \times 45.364\ldots$ ← | Carry on the working with the value from your calculator's memory. |

$= 358 \text{ cm}^2$ (to the nearest cm^2)

> **Exam tip**
>
> Remember to work as accurately as you can and only round your answer at the end of the calculation.

Volume and mass   C

The diagram shows a block of stone of length 1.2 metres.
The cross-section is a rectangle with a trapezium on top.

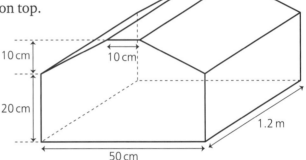

a Calculate:

  i the area of the cross-section

  ii the volume of the block of stone, giving your answer in cubic centimetres.

b The mass of 1 cubic centimetre of the stone is 5 grams.

Calculate the mass of the block. Give your answer in kilograms.

Solution

a **i** Area of rectangle = $50 \times 20 = 1000 \text{ cm}^2$

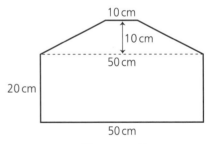

Cross-section

> **Area of a trapezium**
> $= \frac{1}{2} \times$ sum of parallel sides $\times$ perpendicular height

Area of trapezium $= \frac{1}{2} \times (10 + 50) \times 10$

$= \frac{1}{2} \times 60 \times 10 = 300 \text{ cm}^2$

Area of cross-section = $1000 + 300 = 1300 \text{ cm}^2$

> **Exam tip**
>
> Write all dimensions in the same units before using an area or volume formula.

  ii The length of the block of stone = 1.2 m

$= 1.2 \times 100 = 120 \text{ cm}$ | 1 m = 100 cm |

Volume of the block of stone = 1300×120

$= 156\,000 \text{ cm}^3$ | **Volume of a prism** = area of cross-section × length |

b The mass of the block of stone = $156\,000 \times 5 \text{ g} = 780\,000 \text{ g}$

$= 780\,000 \div 1000 = 780 \text{ kg}$ | 1 kg = 1000 g |

Cone and cylinder

B

A cone and a cylinder both have a radius of 5 cm.

The height of the cone is 12 cm.

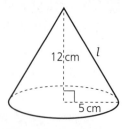

The surface area of the cone and the cylinder are equal.

Calculate the volume of:

a the cone,

b the cylinder,

leaving your answers in terms of π.

Solution

a Volume of the cone $= \frac{1}{3}\pi r^2 h$

$$= \frac{1}{3} \times \pi \times 5^2 \times 12$$

$$= 100\pi \text{ cm}^3$$

b Volume of the cylinder $= \pi r^2 h$

$r = 5$ cm but the height, h, is unknown.

Using surface area of cone = surface area of cylinder

$\pi r l + \pi r^2 = 2\pi r h + 2\pi r^2$

$l + r = 2h + 2r$ ◄——— Dividing every term by πr.

$l - r = 2h$

$\dfrac{l - r}{2} = h$

By Pythagoras,

$l^2 = 12^2 + 5^2$

$l^2 = 144 + 25 = 169$

$l = 13$

$h = \dfrac{l - r}{2}$

$h = \dfrac{13 - 5}{2} = 4$

Volume of the cylinder $= \pi r^2 h = \pi \times 5^2 \times 4 = 100\pi \text{ cm}^3$

> **A cylinder has 2 curved faces + a curved surface:**
>
> $C = 2\pi r$
>
> Area of curved surface $= 2\pi r h$ — h

Hemisphere

A

The volume of a hemisphere is $144\pi \text{ cm}^3$.

Find the total surface area of the hemisphere, giving your answer in terms of π.

Solution

For a hemisphere, $V = \frac{2}{3}\pi r^3$

$$\frac{2}{3}\pi r^3 = 144\pi$$

$$r^3 = \frac{3 \times 144}{2} = 216$$

$$r = \sqrt[3]{216} = 6\,\text{cm}$$

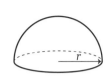

Total surface area of the hemisphere

= curved surface area + area of circular base

$= 2\pi r^2 + \pi r^2 = 3\pi r^2$

$= 3\pi \times 6^2$

$= 108\pi\,\text{cm}^2$

Exam tip

You will be given these formulae in the examination:

- a sphere of radius r has surface area $A = 4\pi r^2$ and volume $V = \frac{4}{3}\pi r^3$
- a pyramid has volume $V = \frac{1}{3}$ base area × height
- a cone of radius r, height h and slant height l has a curved surface area $A = \pi r l$ and volume $V = \frac{1}{3}\pi r^2 h$.

Revise 4.4 Arc lengths and sector areas

Length of an arc

An **arc** is part of the circumference of a circle.

If the angle at the centre is $\theta°$, then

length of arc $= \dfrac{\theta}{360} \times$ circumference

$= \dfrac{\theta}{360} \times 2\pi r$ or $\dfrac{\theta}{360} \times \pi d$

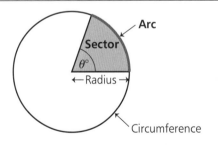

Area of a sector

An area cut off by two radii is a **sector**.

If the angle at the centre is $\theta°$, then

area of sector $= \dfrac{\theta}{360} \times$ area of circle

$= \dfrac{\theta}{360} \times \pi r^2$

Exam tip

It is useful to leave your answers in terms of π until the end of the question.

Worked example

Arc and sector

A

A shape consists of a square of side 6 cm and a sector of a circle as shown.

Calculate:

a the area of the shape

b the perimeter of the shape.

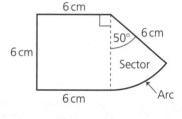

Solution

a   Area of the square $= 6 \times 6 = 36 \, \text{cm}^2$

Area of the sector $= \dfrac{50}{360} \times \pi \times 6^2$

$= 15.7... \, \text{cm}^2$

Total area of the shape $= 15.7... + 36 = 51.7 \, \text{cm}^2$ (to 1 d.p.)

b The perimeter consists of 4 sides of 6 cm + the arc

Perimeter of the shape $= 24 + \dfrac{50}{360} \times \pi \times 12$

$= 24 + 5.23...$

$= 29.2 \, \text{cm}$ (to 1 d.p.)

Practise 4.1 – 4.4

1 For each shape calculate: **i** the perimeter   **ii** the area.

a
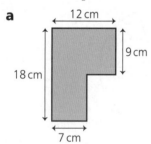

b
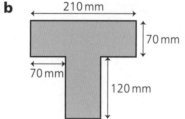

c
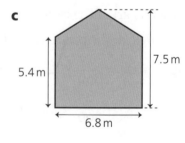

[Grades D–C]

2 a The diameter of a circular pond is 6 metres.

Calculate: **i** the circumference of the pond   **ii** the area of the pond.

b The circumference of a circular plate is 30 centimetres.

Calculate: **i** the radius of the plate   **ii** the area of the plate.

[Grades D–C]

3 Calculate the volume of each prism.

a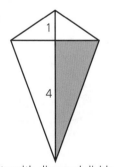

b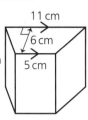

c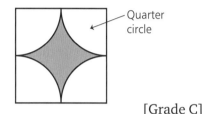

d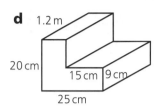

[Grades D–C]

4 The diagram shows a square tile with sides of length 20 cm.

   a Calculate the area of the shaded part.

   b A rectangular wall is 3.2 metres long and 2.4 metres high.
   Find the number of tiles that is needed to cover the wall.

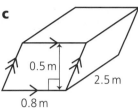
Quarter circle

[Grade C]

5 The diagram shows the dimensions of an oil drum.

   a Sketch a net of the drum.

   b Calculate the total surface area of the drum.
   Give your answer to 2 decimal places.

   c Calculate the capacity of the drum.
   Give your answer in litres.

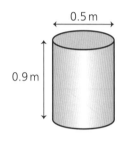

[Grade C]

6 The diagram shows a wooden door.

   ABCD is a rectangle and *CED* is a semicircle.

   a Calculate the area of the door.
   Give your answer in: **i** square metres   **ii** square centimetres.

   b The door is 4 centimetres thick.
   Calculate, in cubic centimetres, the volume of the door.

   c The mass of 1 cubic centimetre of wood is 0.6 gram.
   Calculate the mass of the door. Give your answer in kilograms.

[Grade C]

7 What fraction of each shape is shaded grey?

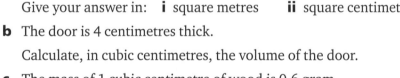

a

Kite with diagonal divided
in the ratio 1 : 4

b

Triangle with base divided
in the ratio 1 : 2

c

Circles with diameters
2 units and 8 units

d

Sectors, centre *O*,
with radii 3 units
and 4 units

[Grades C–B]

8 The table gives the population and land area in **square kilometres** of four islands.

Island	Population	Land area (km²)	Land area per person (m²)
Bermuda	69 000	54	
Malta	408 000	316	
Mauritius	1.3 million	2030	
Australia	2.2×10^7	7.7×10^6	

Copy and complete the table to give the land area per person in **square metres**.

[Grade C]

9 The diagrams show the nets of 3 solids.

The given dimensions are all in centimetres.

a
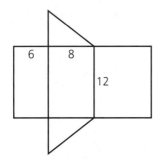

b
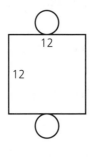

c
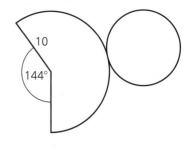

In each case: **i** name the solid

             ii calculate the surface area of the solid

           iii calculate the volume of the solid.

[Grades B–A]

10 Find:

  a the perimeter

  b the area

of the shaded shape.

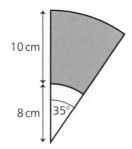

[Grade A]

11 A cone has a volume of $96\pi \, \text{cm}^3$ and a radius of 6 cm.

Calculate:

  a the perpendicular height of the cone

  b the total surface area of the cone, leaving your answer in terms of π.

The volume of a cone is given by $V = \frac{1}{3}\pi r^2 h$.

The area of the curved surface is $A = \pi r l$.

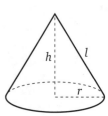

[Grade A]

12 A hemisphere and a cone have the same radius and the same height.

    a Find the ratio of their volumes.

    b Show that the ratio of their total surface areas is $3 : 1 + \sqrt{2}$

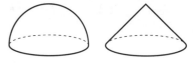

The volume of a cone is given by $V = \frac{1}{3}\pi r^2 h$.

The area of the curved surface of a cone is $A = \pi r l$.

The volume of a sphere is $V = \frac{4}{3}\pi r^3$.

The surface area of a sphere is $A = 4\pi r^2$.

[Grade A]

13 The diagram shows a swimming pool of length 34 m and width 25 m.
A cross-section of the pool, $ABCD$, is a trapezium. $AD = 1.2$ m and $BC = 3.8$ m.

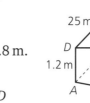

    a Calculate:

      i the area of the trapezium $ABCD$

      ii the number of litres of water in the pool when it is full.

    b $AB = 34.1$ m
The interior surface of the pool is painted. It costs \$2.50 to paint one square metre.
Calculate the cost of painting the pool, correct to the nearest hundred dollars.

    c When the pool is emptied, the water flows through a cylindrical pipe of radius 10 cm.
The water flows along the pipe at a rate of 20 centimetres per second.
Calculate the time taken to empty the pool, giving your answer to the nearest hour.

[Grades B–A]

14 a The volume of a sphere of radius r is $\frac{4}{3}\pi r^3$.
A solid metal sphere has a radius of 2.5 cm.
One cubic centimetre of the metal has a mass of 4.8 grams.
Calculate the mass of the sphere.

    b

      Diagram A   Diagram B

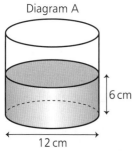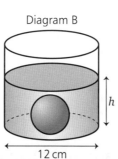

    Diagram A shows a cylinder with a diameter of 12 cm.
It contains water to a depth of 6 cm.
The sphere described in part **a** is placed in the water, as shown in diagram B.
Calculate h, the new depth of water in the cylinder.

    c A different sphere has a mass of 0.5 kg. It is made from the metal described in part **a**.
Calculate the radius of this sphere.

[Grades B–A]

5 Using number

Revise 5.1 Directed numbers

A **directed number** has a positive or negative sign.

A negative sign ($-$) shows that the number is less than zero.

A positive sign ($+$) shows that the number is greater than zero.

When writing positive integers, the $+$ signs can be missed out.

An **integer** is any positive or negative whole number or zero.

Positive integers and **negative integers** can be shown on a number line.

When working with directed numbers, you can use horizontal or vertical number lines to help you.

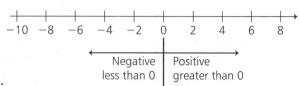

Adding and subtracting positive and negative numbers

There are two uses for $+$ and $-$ signs:

- to show if a number is positive or negative: $+4$ or -4
- to show if you are adding or subtracting: $6 + 4$ or $6 - 4$

You may see both uses of the signs together: $4 - -3$ or $4 - (-3)$

You will then have two signs next to each other.

Use the following rules:

Adding a positive number	+ +	is the same as	+	adding
Adding a negative number	+ −	is the same as	−	subtracting
Subtracting a positive number	− +	is the same as	−	subtracting
Subtracting a negative number	− −	is the same as	+	adding

You will also need to know how to enter calculations on your calculator.

Multiplying and dividing positive and negative numbers

You will need to know the following rules.

For multiplication:

$(+) \times (+) = (+)$

$(+) \times (-) = (-)$

$(-) \times (+) = (-)$

$(-) \times (-) = (+)$

For division:

$(+) \div (+) = (+)$

$(+) \div (-) = (-)$

$(-) \div (+) = (-)$

$(-) \div (-) = (+)$

Another way of remembering this is:

signs the same, positive answer

signs different, negative answer.

Worked examples

Temperature calculations

E

The table shows the maximum and minimum temperatures of some planets in our Solar System.

a Using your knowledge of positive and negative integers, copy and complete the table.

Planet	Minimum temperature (°C)	Maximum temperature (°C)	Difference in temperatures (°C)
Earth	−89	71	
Mercury	−184	465	
Mars	−140	20	

b Find the mean minimum temperature of the three planets.

Solution

a Earth: Difference $= 71 - -89 = 71 + 89 = 160\,°C$

   Mercury: Difference $= 465 - -184 = 465 + 184 = 649\,°C$

   Mars: Difference $= 20 - -140 = 20 + 140 = 160\,°C$

b Mean minimum temperature $= \dfrac{-89 + -184 + -140}{3}$

$= -138\,°C$ (to the nearest degree)

Directed number calculations

C

Work out:

a $-3 - (-4)^2$

c $\dfrac{-2 - 4 \times -1}{2}$

b $-2(3 - 4)$

d $3 + \left(\frac{1}{2}\right)^2 \times -\frac{1}{3}$

Solution

a $-3 - (-4)^2 = -3 - 16 = -19$

c $\dfrac{-2 - 4 \times -1}{2} = \dfrac{-2 + 4}{2} = \dfrac{2}{2} = 1$

b $-2(3 - 4) = -2 \times (-1) = 2$

d $3 + \left(\frac{1}{2}\right)^2 \times -\frac{1}{3} = 3 + \frac{1}{4} \times -\frac{1}{3} = 3 - \frac{1}{12} = 2\frac{11}{12}$

Revise 5.2 Time and money

Digital and analogue displays

Some displays are **digital**. They show readings as numbers.

For example, the **odometer** in a car shows how far it has travelled: $\boxed{0}\boxed{1}\boxed{7}\boxed{4}\boxed{3}\boxed{2}$

The reading shown is 17 432 km.

Scales for weighing can be digital or **analogue**.

Analogue scales have a moving hand to show the weight.

These scales both show a reading of 3.7 kg.

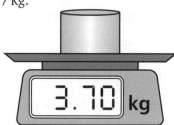

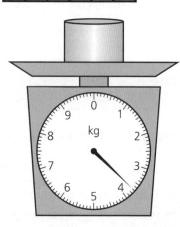

12-hour and 24-hour clocks

Time can use the 12-hour or the 24-hour clock.

The 12-hour clock times use 'am' to indicate morning and 'pm' to show an afternoon time.

24-hour clock times use times 13, 14, 15, … to represent pm times. In the 24-hour clock, hours and minutes are not separated by a colon, and all times are written using four digits.

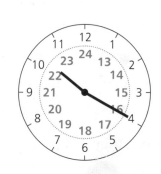

To change pm times to the 24-hour clock, add 12 to the hours.

10.20pm is 2220.

But 3.45am is written as 0345, as the hours before noon are the same in both systems.

Timetables are usually written using the 24-hour clock.

Calculating with time

To calculate the interval between two times:

1 Calculate the number of minutes to the next hour (o'clock).

2 Then calculate the number of complete hours.

3 Then work out the number of minutes remaining.

The first worked example shows how to do this.

Calculating with money

Bills

A bill usually gives the unit price of an item.

You must multiply the quantity by the unit price before finding the total bill.

Currency conversion

To **convert** from one currency to another you use a conversion rate.

A conversion rate tells you how much of one currency you receive for 1 unit of the other.

> **Exam tip**
>
> Do not round off your calculation until the final answer.

≡ Worked examples

Journey calculation   E

Corbie needs to travel from Paris to Berlin.

He looks at the train timetable.

Destination							
Paris	0641	0744	0841	0949	1241	1349	1641
Köln	1026		1226		1626		2026
Frankfurt		1153		1358		1758	
Berlin	1451	1603	1651	1808	2051	2208	0051+

All trains from Paris to Berlin go via Köln or Frankfurt.

The journey times from Paris to Köln are all the same.

So are the journey times from Paris to Frankfurt, Köln to Berlin and Frankfurt to Berlin.

a Corbie needs to be in Berlin by 4.30pm.

   Which train should he catch?

b Calculate how long the journey takes.

c Is the journey quicker via Köln or via Frankfurt, and by how much?

d Corbie catches a train back to Paris, via Köln, leaving Berlin at 2246.

If the journey times are the same as the outward journey, at what time will the train reach:

i Köln

ii Paris?

Solution

a 4.30pm is 1630.

He must catch the 0744, arriving at 1603.

b The 0744 arrives at 1603.

From 0744 to 0800 = 16 minutes

From 0800 to 1600 = 8 hours

From 1600 to 1603 = 3 minutes

Total time = 8 hours 19 minutes

c The journey via Frankfurt = 8 h 19 min

The journey via Köln: The 0641 arrives at 1451.

From 0641 to 0700 = 19 minutes

From 0700 to 1400 = 7 hours

From 1400 to 1451 = 51 minutes

Total time = 7 hours 70 minutes

= 8 hours 10 minutes ← As 70 minutes = 1 hour 10 minutes.

The journey via Köln is 9 minutes quicker.

d The journey time from Köln to Berlin:

1026 to 1451:

1026 to 1100 = 34 minutes

1100 to 1400 = 3 hours

1400 to 1451 = 51 minutes

Total time = 3 hours 95 minutes

= 4 hours 35 minutes ← As 95 minutes = 1 hour 35 minutes.

i So, a train leaving Berlin at 2246 arrives at Köln at:

22 h 46 min

+ 4 h 35 min

26 h 81 min

= 27 h 21 min ← As 81 minutes = 1 hour 21 minutes.

= 0321 the following day ← As there are 24 hours in a day.

ii The journey time from Paris to Berlin via Köln is 8 hours 10 minutes.

So the 2246 from Berlin will reach Paris at

$$\begin{array}{r} 22\text{ h } 46\text{ min} \\ +\ 08\text{ h } 10\text{ min} \\ \hline 30\text{ h } 56\text{ min} \end{array}$$

= 0656 the next day ◄——— As there are 24 hours in a day.

Working out a bill

E

Complete this decorator's bill:

Materials		
1.5 kg of filler	at $0.98 per kg	= $
4 litres of undercoat	at $2.20 per litre	= $
6.5 litres topcoat	at $2.56 per litre	= $
3 litres white emulsion	at $1.75 per litre	= $
1.5 litres wood stain	at $2.60 per litre	= $

Labour

To prepare walls and ceiling:

To apply 1 coat of undercoat, 2 coats of topcoat

2 coats emulsion to ceiling

2 coats of wood stain to woodwork:

8.5 hours	at $15 per hour	= $
TOTAL		**= $**

Solution

Materials		
1.5 kg of filler	at $0.98 per kg	= $1.47
4 litres of undercoat	at $2.20 per litre	= $8.80
6.5 litres topcoat	at $2.56 per litre	= $16.64
3 litres white emulsion	at $1.75 per litre	= $5.25
1.5 litres wood stain	at $2.60 per litre	= $3.90

Labour

To prepare walls and ceiling:

To apply 1 coat of undercoat, 2 coats of topcoat

2 coats emulsion to ceiling

2 coats of wood stain to woodwork:

8.5 hours	at $15 per hour	= $127.50
TOTAL		**= $163.56**

> Multiply number of units (kg, litres, hours) by the unit cost.

Currency conversion

E | D | C

One Singapore dollar is worth 4.26 Danish kroner.

a Change 350 Singapore dollars into Danish kroner.

b Change 1000 Danish kroner into Singapore dollars.

c An item costs 36 dollars in Singapore and 150 kroner in Denmark.

In which country is it cheaper?

Solution

a 1 dollar = 4.26 kroner

350 dollars = 350 × 4.26 = 1491 kroner

b 4.26 kroner = 1 dollar

$1 \text{ kroner} = \dfrac{1}{4.26} \text{ dollar}$

$1000 \text{ kroner} = 1000 \times \dfrac{1}{4.26} = 234.74 \text{ dollars}$

c You can change 36 dollars into kroner or 150 kroner into dollars.

36 dollars = 36 × 4.26 = 153.36 kroner

The item is cheaper in Denmark.

Revise 5.3 Percentages

Percentages of a quantity

To find a percentage of a quantity you can change the percentage to a fraction or a decimal:

A fraction:

42% of $19

$= \dfrac{42}{100} \times \$19$

$= \$7.98$

A decimal:

42% of $19

$= 0.42 \times \$19$

$= \$7.98$

Exam tip

Make sure you know how to input fractions into your calculator using the fraction key.

You should be able to work these out on a calculator.

Write one quantity as a percentage of another

To write one quantity as a percentage of another:

- first, write it as a fraction

- then multiply by 100 to get a percentage.

Percentage increase and decrease

When a quantity goes up, it is called an **increase**.

When a quantity goes down, it is called a **decrease**.

When the value of an item increases, it **appreciates**.

When the value of an item decreases, it **depreciates**.

Percentage increases or decreases are calculated as percentages of the original amount.

So the original value is always 100%.

Calculating the new amount

If an article increases in value, add the percentage to 100%.

For example, if an antique appreciates by 12%, its value increases from 100% to
(100% + 12%) = 112%.

If an article decreases in value, subtract the percentage from 100%.

For example, if a bicycle depreciates by 24%, its value decreases from 100% to
(100% − 24%) = 76%.

Calculating the percentage

All percentage increases and decreases are calculated as percentages of the original value.

First, calculate the new amount as a percentage of the original amount.

Calculate the change from 100%.

Reverse percentages

You use reverse percentages to calculate the original amount.

For example, a coat is reduced by 40% in a sale. The sale price is $51.

This represents (100% − 40%) = 60% of the original price.

So the original price × 0.6 = $51. ◄——— 60% = 0.6 as a decimal.

Original price = $51 ÷ 0.6 = $85.

Worked examples

Age ranges of a group of people as percentages   D

An airline records the ages of people on a plane.

a What percentage of the passengers are over 30 years old?

b The airline wants to encourage more young people to fly
with them.

  i How many passengers were under 30?

  ii Out of those under 30, what percentage were more
than 20 years old?

Age (years)	Frequency
0 < x ⩽ 10	1
10 < x ⩽ 20	4
20 < x ⩽ 30	29
30 < x ⩽ 40	54
40 < x ⩽ 50	27
50 < x ⩽ 60	11
60 < x ⩽ 70	5

Solution

a There are $1 + 4 + 29 + 54 + 27 + 11 + 5 = 131$ passengers.

$54 + 27 + 11 + 5 = 97$ passengers are over 30 years old.

$\frac{97}{131} \times 100 = 74.0458\ldots$

$\qquad = 74.0\%$ (to 1 d.p.)

b **i** $1 + 4 + 29 = 34$ are under 30.

$\quad$ **ii** $\frac{29}{34} \times 100 = 85.2941\ldots$

$\qquad\qquad = 85.3\%$ (to 1 d.p.) were at least 20 years old.

> **Exam tip**
>
> If necessary, round answers to 1 decimal place.

A new amount from a percentage decrease

$\boxed{D}$

Tak buys a car for $4200.

During the next year, it decreases in value by 12%.

Find the value of the car after this decrease.

Solution

The decrease is 12% of $4200.

The new value of the car is: 88% of $4200 $\longleftarrow$ $\boxed{100\% - 12\% = 88\%}$

$\qquad\qquad\qquad = 0.88 \times \$4200$ $\longleftarrow$ $\boxed{88\% = 0.88 \text{ as a decimal}}$

$\qquad\qquad\qquad = \$3696$

Percentage increase

$\boxed{C}$

The population of a village increased from 2056 to 2345.

Calculate the percentage increase.

Solution:

The increase is $2345 - 2056 = 289$

The percentage increase is $\frac{289}{2056} \times 100 = 14.0564\ldots$

$= 14.1\%$ (to 1 d.p.)

> **Exam tip**
>
> - Remember to divide by the original amount or number.
> - Whenever a value changes, the change is given as a percentage of the original value.

A new amount from a percentage increase

$\boxed{B}$

Raul gets a pay rise of 7%.

After the pay rise he receives $37 022 per year.

What did he earn before the pay rise?

Solution

His pay rise of 7% means he receives $(100\% + 7\%) = 107\%$ of his previous salary.

Original salary $\times 1.07 = \$37\,022.$ $\longleftarrow$ $\boxed{107\% = 1.07 \text{ as a decimal}}$

Original salary $= \dfrac{\$37\,022}{1.07} = \$34\,600.$

Revise 5.4 Personal finance

Earnings

Wages

Some people are paid a **weekly wage**.

They have an **hourly rate of pay**, and a number of hours a week they have to work.

They can work **overtime**, which is usually paid at a higher rate.

It might be paid at **time-and-a-half** ($1\frac{1}{2}$ times the normal hourly rate).

Or it might be paid at **double time** (twice the normal hourly rate).

Salaries

Some people are paid an **annual salary**.

They get a fixed amount of money for a year's work.

The money is paid monthly, so the annual salary is divided by 12 and that amount is paid every month.

People on salaries are not usually paid overtime.

They sometimes get a **bonus** at the end of the year.

Taxes

People pay taxes so that the government can pay for public services.

The taxes depend on which country you live in.

Income tax is tax paid on money you earn.

Buying and selling

Profit and loss

If you sell something for more than you paid for it, you make a **profit**.

If you sell it for less than you paid for it, you make a **loss**.

Discount

A discount is an amount of money taken off the price of goods. It is often written as a percentage.

> **Exam tip**
>
> Whenever a value changes, the change is given as a percentage of the original value.

VAT

Many countries charge Value Added Tax (VAT), sales tax or consumption tax on goods.

The level of this tax varies, but is usually around 15%.

Hire purchase

Sometimes you buy goods on hire purchase. This is a useful way of buying items and paying for them over a number of months. You pay some money to start with, called a **deposit**, followed by a number of monthly **instalments**. Buying by hire purchase usually costs more than paying all at once.

Interest

Simple interest

When you invest money in a bank, they usually pay you **interest**.

The formula for the interest is:

$$I = \frac{PRT}{100}$$

where P is the **principal** (the amount you invest), R is the **rate** of interest (the percentage of the principal paid each year) and T is the time in years that you invest the money.

Compound interest

Most banks pay **compound interest**.

With compound interest, the first year's interest is added to the principal.

So the second year's interest is calculated on a bigger principal.

It continues in this way every year.

You also pay compound interest on loans, including credit cards.

The final amount, F, is given by the formula:

$$F = P\left(1 + \frac{R}{100}\right)^T$$

where P is the principal invested, R is the rate of interest and T is the time in years.

 Worked examples

Income tax calculation

D

Benny earns $15 835 per year.

He earns $12 000 tax free, and pays income tax at 24% on the remainder.

How much tax does he pay per year?

Solution

His taxable income = income − tax-free income

Taxable income = $15 835 − $12 000 = $3835

Income tax = 24% of taxable income

$$= 24\% \text{ of } \$3835$$

$$= 0.24 \times \$3835$$

$$= \$920.40$$

Profit and VAT calculation

[C]

a Mustapha buys a car for $4000 and sells it for $4200.

Calculate his percentage profit.

b The price of $4200 included 20% VAT.

Calculate the amount of VAT.

Solution

a Mustapha's profit is $200.

His percentage profit $= \frac{200}{4000} \times 100 = 5\%$

b Price including VAT $= 100\% + 20\% = 120\%$

Original price $\times 1.20 = \$4200$

Original price $= \$4200 \div 1.20$

$= \$3500$

So the VAT $= \$4200 - \$3500 = \$700$

> **Exam tip**
>
> Make sure you read the question carefully, as simple interest and compound interest are calculated differently.

Compound interest

[C]

Tak has $5000 to invest.

She invests it for 3 years at 2.1% compound interest.

What is the value of the investment after 3 years?

Solution

$$F = P\left(1 + \frac{R}{100}\right)^{T}$$

$$F = 5000\left(1 + \frac{2.1}{100}\right)^{3}$$

$F = \$5321.66$ (to 2 d.p.)

The investment is worth $5321.66

Practise 5.1 – 5.4

1 The table shows the mean monthly temperatures for two different places in Canada.

	Jan	Feb	Mar	April	May	June	July	Aug	Sept	Oct	Nov	Dec
Alert	−30 °C	−31 °C	−30 °C	−22 °C	−8 °C	2 °C	5 °C	3 °C	−6 °C	−15 °C	−23 °C	−29 °C
Niagara Falls	−9 °C	−8 °C	−1 °C	2 °C	12 °C	15 °C	21 °C	19 °C	11 °C	10 °C	2 °C	−4 °C

a Write down the maximum and minimum monthly temperatures for **i** Alert and **ii** Niagara Falls.

b What are the differences in temperatures between the two places in **i** February and **ii** May?

c In which month are the temperature differences **i** the greatest **ii** the least?

[Grade E]

2 Work out the following:

a $+8 - (-6) + (-9)$

c $8 - 2 \times 3 + (-10)$

b $-24 \div 9 \, (-8)$

d $6 \times (-3) - (-2) \times (-4)$

[Grade E]

3 a 1 Bahraini dinar is worth 2.59 Australian dollars.

Find the value of 225 Bahraini dinars in Australian dollars.

b 1 Indian rupee is worth 7.66 Armenian dram.

Find the value of 2000 Armenian drams in Indian rupees.

[Grades E–D]

4 Maiya buys a CD.

There are 16 tracks on the CD.

The length of each track is given below.

2 min 35 s	3 min 12 s	4 min 7 s	2 min 11 s	2 min 51 s	3 min 12 s
3 min 17 s	2 min 34 s	3 min 19 s	4 min 1 s	4 min 5 s	2 min 11 s
3 min 5 s	3 min 42 s	2 min 44 s	5 min 2 s		

There is a 2-second pause between each track.

How long does it take to play the entire CD?

[Grade E]

5 Which is greater, and by how much: 35% of $40 or 65% of $22?

[Grade D]

6 Maria earns $67 500 per annum. She earns $34 000 tax free, and then pays income tax at 18% on the remainder.

Calculate how much tax she pays.

[Grade D]

7 An aeroplane flies from city A to B, and then on to C.

The flight from A to B takes 2 hours 27 minutes.

The plane waits at B for 42 minutes before taking off.

The flight from B to C takes 3 hours 18 minutes.

Complete the timetable below for three such flights.

	Flight 1	Flight 2	Flight 3
Depart A	0836		
Arrive B		1325	
Depart B			
Arrive C			0145

[Grade E]

8 Griselda is using this recipe:

4 skinned, boned chicken breasts, about 125 g each

20 g butter, melted

15 g clear honey

15 ml lemon juice

15 ml balsamic vinegar

The cost of the ingredients is shown in the table:

Ingredient	Price	Unit
Chicken breasts	$17.50	1 kg
Butter	$1.45	250 g
Honey	$1.20	330 g
Lemon juice	$1.45	500 ml
Balsamic vinegar	$1.20	250 ml

Calculate the cost of the ingredients used in the recipe.

[Grade C]

9 Millie bought a bag in this sale.

She paid $14.95

a What was the original price of the bag?

b The next day, all items were sold at half the original price.

How much more would Millie have saved if she had waited until the next day to buy the bag?

[Grades C–B]

10 Find the values of:

a $\dfrac{-5 - 7 + 2}{2 - -3}$

b $\dfrac{(-3)^2 - (-2)^2}{4 \times (-3 - 2)}$

c $\left(-\dfrac{1}{5}\right)^3 \times (4^2 + 3^2)$

d $(3 \div -4 \times 2) \div ((-10 + 3) \div 2)$

[Grades E–C]

11 a Marco scored 39 out of 60 in a test. Calculate his mark as a percentage.

b To pass the test, you needed to score 70%.

How many marks out of 60 did you need to pass?

[Grade E]

12 Carlos is starting a business.

He borrows $6000 from a loan company.

The loan company charges 4% per year compound interest.

How much interest will Carlos have paid after 3 years?

[Grade C]

13 a The population of a city is 45 240.

It is predicted that over the next ten years the population will increase by 35%.

Calculate the predicted population ten years from now.

b The population has increased by 30% over the last ten years.

What was the population 10 years ago?

[Grades B–C]

14 I invest $800 in a bank which pays 4.1% per year compound interest.

I leave the money there for three years.

a How much do I have in the bank after three years?

b What rate of simple interest would give the same amount?

[Grades C–A]

15 A store sells computers.

The store owner makes a profit of 30%.

The selling price for the computer is $442.

a How much does the store pay for the computer originally?

b In a sale, the store reduces the price by 20%.

What is the store's percentage profit in the sale?

[Grade B]

6 Statistics

Learning outcomes

After this chapter you should be able to:

- collect and tabulate data, and interpret information in tables and statistical diagrams
- construct and use bar charts and pictograms
- construct and use pie charts and scatter diagrams, draw a line of best fit and understand correlation
- calculate the mean, median, mode and range for discrete data and from frequency tables
- calculate an estimate of the mean and identify the modal class for grouped and continuous data
- construct and use cumulative frequency diagrams
- estimate and interpret the median, percentiles, quartiles and interquartile range
- construct and read histograms with equal and unequal intervals.

Revise 6.1 Statistical diagrams

Collecting and interpreting data

Tally charts

A **tally chart** is a method of showing a set of data.

Tallies are recorded in blocks of 5, making it easy to find the total, or **frequency**, for each category.

Tally charts are also used for **grouping** data, as in this example.

Test score	Tally	Frequency
41–50	ЖН II	7
51–60	ЖН ЖН IIII	14
61–70	ЖН ЖН ЖН ЖН I	21
71–80	ЖН II	7
Total		49

Exam tip

Always add up the frequency column and check that the total is equal to the number of elements of data.

Two-way tables

A **two-way table** is used when you need to show two different pieces of information.

The test scores above could be sorted by gender:

Score	41–50	51–60	61–70	71–80
Male	3	9	8	4
Female	4	5	13	3

Bar charts and pictograms

Bar charts

A **bar chart** has parallel bars or columns of the same width, with a space between them.

Each bar shows the quantity of a different category of data.

Bar charts can be used for numeric (or **quantitative**) data or descriptive (or **qualitative**) data.

Pictograms

A **pictogram** is a way of displaying qualitative data.

The data is displayed by using pictures, and a key shows the quantity that each picture represents.

The data can be shown in a bar chart or a pictogram.

The table below shows the colours of cars in a car park.

Colour	Frequency
Red	22
Blue	13
Black	28
Silver	17

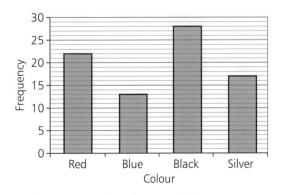

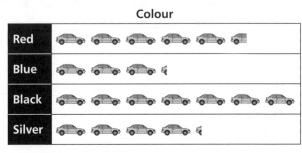

Key: represents 4 cars.

Pie charts and scatter diagrams

Pie charts

A **pie chart** is circular in shape. Pie charts show frequencies as proportions.

Pie charts are useful when representing a sample, where proportions are more important than the actual frequencies.

To construct a pie chart, the angle at the centre, 360°, must be divided into equal parts for each entry in the survey.

Scatter diagrams

Scatter diagrams are used to compare two sets of data, for example, the heights and ages of children.

They are constructed by plotting points on a graph.

Scatter diagrams are used to see if there is a connection, or **correlation**, between two sets of data.

A **positive correlation** means that high values of one feature are matched by high values of the other feature.

A **negative correlation** means that high values of one feature are matched by low values of the other feature.

Line of best fit

When a scatter diagram shows correlation, you can draw a **line of best fit**. This is a straight line that goes between the points, passing as close as possible to all of them.

When the points are very close to a line of best fit, it is called a **strong correlation**. If the points are not all close to a line of best fit, it is called a **weak correlation**.

Mean, median, mode and range

An average is a single figure that represents a set of data.

You need to know three different averages: **mean**, **median** and **mode**.

You also need to be able to find the **range**. The range is not an average.

Mean

The mean is a way of calculating how much each value would be if they were shared out equally.

To find the mean, you add all the values together, and then share them out equally by dividing.

$$\text{Mean} = \frac{\text{sum of all the values}}{\text{total number of values}}$$

Median

The median is the middle value when the data is put in order.

The median can be a useful average because it has the same amount of data on either side of it.

The position of the median, m, is given by $\frac{n+1}{2}$, where n is the size of the data set.

If there is an even number of values in the data set, then there will be a middle pair of values.

The median is the mean of the middle pair.

> **Exam tip**
>
> Remember to order the data to find the median.

Mode

The mode is the most frequent value or number, or the value with the highest **frequency**.

The mode can be called the **modal** number.

> **Exam tip**
>
> Remember there can be more than one mode, or no mode at all.

Range

The range tells you how spread out the data are.

  Range = largest number − smallest number

The range is a single value.

Frequency tables

If the data is presented in a frequency table, take care that you interpret it correctly to find averages.

For example, the table shows the number of shots a golfer takes on each hole.

Number of shots	Frequency
1	0
2	2
3	3
4	5
5	7
6	1
Total	18

To find the *mean*, add up the number of shots from all 18 holes:

Number of shots	Frequency	The calculations in this column are very important	Number of shots × frequency
1	0	He scores a hole in 1 shot on 0 occasions. $0 \times 1 =$	0
2	2	He scores a hole in 2 shots on 2 occasions. $2 \times 2 =$	4
3	3	He scores a hole in 3 shots on 3 occasions. $3 \times 3 =$	9
4	5	He scores a hole in 4 shots on 5 occasions. $5 \times 4 =$	20
5	7	He scores a hole in 5 shots on 7 occasions. $7 \times 5 =$	35
6	1	He scores a hole in 6 shots on 1 occasion. $1 \times 6 =$	6
Total	18	Altogether he takes 74 shots	74

He takes 74 shots over 18 holes, so the *mean* is $\frac{74}{18} = 4.1$ (1 d.p.)

The median will be in the $\frac{18 + 1}{2} = 9.5$th position.

To find the 9th and 10th numbers think of the data as written out in order.

There are two 2s, three 3s, five 4s, seven 5s and one 6.

So the 2s are in positions 1 and 2, the 3s are in positions 3, 4, 5, the 4s are in positions 6, 7, 8, 9, 10.

So the 9th and 10th numbers are both 4.

The *median* is 4.

The *mode* is the number with the highest frequency, which is 5.

The range is $6 - 2 = 4$, as his biggest score was 6 and the smallest was 2.

Worked examples

Pie charts

E

The table shows the colours of cars in a car park.

Colour	Frequency
Red	22
Blue	13
Black	28
Silver	17

Show these results in a pie chart.

Solution

Adding the frequencies shows that there are 80 cars.

Each car occupies $360° \div 80 = 4.5°$.

So the angles for each colour are:

Colour	Frequency		Angle
Red	22	× 4.5° =	99°
Blue	13	× 4.5° =	58.5°
Black	28	× 4.5° =	126°
Silver	17	× 4.5° =	76.5°
Total	80	× 4.5° =	360°

Exam tip

Before drawing the pie chart, make sure the angles add up to 360°.

A pie chart showing the colours:

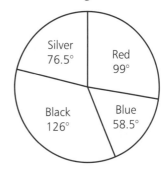

Scatter diagrams

D

Here are the heights and hand spans of nine 16-year-old males:

	A	B	C	D	E	F	G	H	I
Height (cm)	156	189	162	179	187	159	177	184	165
Hand span (cm)	14	16	15	15.5	16	14.5	14.5	16	15

a Draw a scatter diagram to show this information.

b Describe the correlation between height and hand span.

c Which person has got a small hand span for his height?

d Another 16-year-old male is 170 cm tall. Draw a line of best fit and use it to predict his hand span.

Solution

a

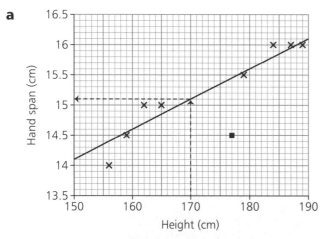

Exam tip

When you draw a line of best fit, make sure the line has approximately equal numbers of points on either side.

b There is a weak positive correlation.

c The male marked with a square has a small hand span for his height as the point is below others representing similar heights. This is called an outlier. It is male G.

d The male with a height of 170 cm should have a hand span of approximately 15.1 cm, shown by the arrowed line.

Calculating the mean, median, mode and range for a set of data $\boxed{\text{E}}$

For this set of data,

7 11 6 9 12 4 5 9 8 6 2 10 11 6 8 9 11 5 7 3

find:

a the mean   **b** the median   **c** the mode   **d** the range.

Solution

a Add up the numbers on your calculator. The sum is 149.

There are 20 numbers in this set of data, so divide the sum by 20:

mean $= 149 \div 20 = 7.45$

b To find the median put the numbers in order:

2 3 4 5 5 6 6 6 7 ⑦ 8 8 9 9 9 10 11 11 11 12

There are 20 numbers, so the middle one is in the $\dfrac{20 + 1}{2} = 10.5$th position.

The 10th number is 7 and the 11th number is 8 (circled).

The median is $\dfrac{7 + 8}{2} = 7.5$

c There are three modes: 6, 9 and 11, as there are three of each.

d The range is the difference between the largest number and the smallest number: $12 - 2 = 10$.

> **Exam tip**
>
> - When you add up the numbers, cross them out lightly as you work through them.
> - Do the same when you put them in order to find the median.

Revise 6.2 Statistical measures

Continuous and discrete data

Grouping data

Discrete data can only take on certain values, for example, the number of people in a store.

Continuous data can take on any value, for example, the mass of a parcel.

The method of grouping is different for discrete data and continuous data.

Discrete data		Continuous data	
Number of people in a store each day in February	Frequency	Mass of a parcel, m (kg)	Frequency
1–5	5	$0 < m \leqslant 5$	3
6–10	9	$5 < m \leqslant 10$	6
11–15	8	$10 < m \leqslant 15$	9
16–20	6	$15 < m \leqslant 20$	5

The modal class

When data is put into groups, you cannot find the mode, because you do not have each individual piece of data.

Instead, you can find the most common group. This is called the **modal class**.

The modal class for the number of people in the store is 6–10, as this is the group with the highest frequency.

The modal class for the mass of a parcel is $10\,\text{kg} < m \leqslant 15\,\text{kg}$, as this is the group with the highest frequency.

Estimating the mean for grouped data

For grouped data, you cannot find the mean because you do not have each individual piece of data.

You must assume that all the data in a group is equal to the middle value for that group.

The middle value is calculated by finding the mean of the **class boundaries** (the greatest and smallest values in a class).

Cumulative frequency

Cumulative frequency tables

A cumulative frequency table records the quantity of data up to a given value.

Frequency table	
Height, h (cm)	Frequency
$130 \leqslant h < 140$	3
$140 \leqslant h < 150$	15
$150 \leqslant h < 160$	14
$160 \leqslant h < 170$	4

Cumulative frequency table	
Height, h (cm)	Cumulative frequency
$h < 130$	0
$h < 140$	3
$h < 150$	18
$h < 160$	32
$h < 170$	36

Cumulative frequency diagrams

The information in the cumulative frequency table can be plotted on a graph.

The graph is called a cumulative frequency diagram.

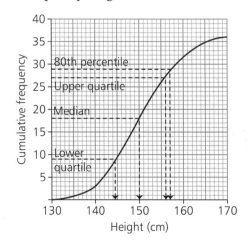

Medians, quartiles and range, percentiles

The **median** is the halfway value in an ordered list of data.

The **lower quartile** is the value one quarter of the way from the lowest value.

The **upper quartile** is the value three quarters of the way from the lowest value.

A **percentile** is the value at a given percentage of the way from the lowest value.

In this example, the median is the value of the 18th item, as $\frac{1}{2}$ of 36 is 18. The median is 150 cm.

The lower quartile is the value of the 9th item, as $\frac{1}{4}$ of 36 = 9. The lower quartile is 144.5 cm.

The upper quartile is the value of the 27th item, as $\frac{3}{4}$ of 36 = 27. The upper quartile is 156 cm.

With 36 items of data, the 80th percentile is the value of the 29th item, as 80% of 36 = 28.8. The 80th percentile is 157 cm.

Cumulative frequency diagrams are useful for analysing the spread of data.

The **interquartile range** tells you the range of the middle half of the data, as it excludes the greatest and smallest quarters.

The interquartile range is the difference between the upper and lower quartiles.

So the interquartile range is 156 – 144.5 = 11.5 cm.

> **Exam tip**
>
> The interquartile range is a single value.

Histograms

A **histogram** is used when data is grouped into classes with different widths.

A histogram represents the data in bars.

The frequency is indicated by the *area* of the bar.

The vertical axis shows the frequency density.

$$\text{Frequency density} = \frac{\text{frequency}}{\text{interval width}}$$

So the actual frequency can be calculated by multiplying the frequency density by the interval width.

Worked examples

Estimating the mean for grouped data

Calculate an estimate of the mean number of words in a sentence in a newspaper article.

Number of words in a sentence	Frequency
1–5	3
6–10	8
11–15	5
16–20	2

Solution

The table below shows the middle values for each group.

Number of words in a sentence	Frequency	Middle value	Middle value × frequency
1–5	3	3	9
6–10	8	8	64
11–15	5	13	65
16–20	2	18	36
Total	**18**		**174**

Estimate of mean $= \dfrac{174}{18} = 9.7$ (to 1 d.p.)

Histograms

A

The table shows the heights of 100 people.

Show this information in a histogram.

Height, h (cm)	Frequency, f
$130 < h \leq 150$	2
$150 < h \leq 170$	5
$170 < h \leq 180$	36
$180 < h \leq 185$	27
$185 < h \leq 190$	13

Solution

Add two columns to the table to show the interval width, w, and the frequency density, $\dfrac{f}{w}$.

Height, h (cm)	Frequency, f	Interval width, w	Frequency density, $\dfrac{f}{w}$
$130 < h \leq 150$	2	20	0.1
$150 < h \leq 170$	5	20	0.25
$170 < h \leq 180$	36	10	3.6
$180 < h \leq 185$	27	5	5.4
$185 < h \leq 190$	13	5	2.6

Then draw the histogram:

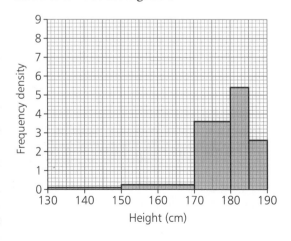

Exam tip

- Bar charts show frequency on the vertical axis. Histograms show frequency density on the vertical axis.

- The area of a bar on a histogram represents the frequency.

Practise 6.1 – 6.2

1 Manfred and Thomas have a long jump competition. They both jump four times.

Here are their distances, in metres.

	Jump 1 (m)	Jump 2 (m)	Jump 3 (m)	Jump 4 (m)
Manfred	4.12	3.98	3.88	4.06
Thomas	3.87	3.89	4.14	4.02

  a Who had the larger mean distance, and by how much?

  b Who had the larger range of distances, and by how much?

  c Who had the larger median, and by how much?

  d Who do you think did better overall? Give your reasons.

  e The winner is the person with the longest jump. Who won?

[Grades E–C]

2 a Six parcels have a mean weight of 4.5 kg. What is the total weight of the parcels?

  b A seventh parcel weighs 5.2 kg. Calculate the mean weight of all seven parcels.

[Grades D–C]

3 This pie chart shows the favourite type of film of
students in a class:

  a Which type was chosen by exactly $\frac{1}{4}$ of the class?

  b The angle for romance films is 60°.
  Four children chose romance as their favourite.

  The angle for comedy films is 135°. How many chose comedy?

  c How many children are there in the class?

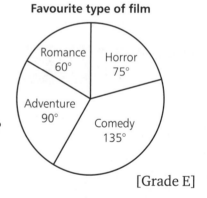

Favourite type of film

[Grade E]

4 In a town there are 20 houses for sale.

The table below shows the number of bedrooms and the price of each house.

Number of bedrooms	2	4	1	3	2	3	4	1	3	2
Price of house, x ($1000s)	85	124	67	95	90	101	132	60	97	88
Number of bedrooms	4	3	2	3	4	1	3	4	3	2
Price of house, x ($1000s)	124	98	84	90	115	62	88	144	91	78

  a i Use the information to complete the table:

  ii Use the table to draw a pie chart showing
  the number of bedrooms.

Number of bedrooms	Frequency
1	
2	
3	
4	

b **i** Complete the table showing the price of the houses:

Price of house, x ($1000s)	Frequency
$60 \leqslant x < 80$	
$80 \leqslant x < 100$	
$100 \leqslant x < 120$	
$120 \leqslant x < 140$	
$140 \leqslant x < 160$	

    ii Show this information in a histogram.

c **i** Draw a scatter graph to show the number of bedrooms and the price of a house.

    ii Describe the correlation between the number of bedrooms and the price of a house.

[Grades E–D]

5 Ravinder spins a five-sided spinner fifty times. The table shows the frequency of his scores:

Score	Frequency
1	11
2	7
3	11
4	
5	8

a Calculate the frequency for a score of 4.

b Calculate:

    i the mean score

    ii the median score

    iii the modal score

    iv the range of scores.

[Grade D]

6 A store owner kept a record of how much customers spent on their shopping.

The results are shown in the table:

Amount spent, x ($)	$0 < x \leqslant 10$	$10 < x \leqslant 20$	$20 < x \leqslant 30$	$30 < x \leqslant 40$	$40 < x \leqslant 50$	$50 < x \leqslant 60$
Number of customers	25	28	12	9	5	1

a Write down the modal class.

b Calculate an estimate of the mean.

c Construct a cumulative frequency table to show the information.

d Use a scale of 2 cm to represent $10 on the horizontal axis and 2 cm to represent 20 customers on the vertical axis to draw a cumulative frequency diagram.

e Use your cumulative frequency diagram to find:

    i the median amount of money spent

    ii the interquartile range

    iii the percentage of customers spending $35 or more.

[Grades D–B]

7 The table shows the ages of the passengers on an aeroplane:

Age, x (years)	$0 < x \leqslant 10$	$10 < x \leqslant 20$	$20 < x \leqslant 40$	$40 < x \leqslant 70$	$70 < x \leqslant 80$
Number of passengers	6	29	56	48	11

The information is shown in the histogram:

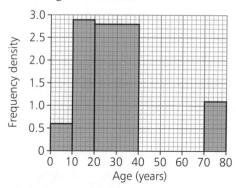

a The bar to represent the ages of $40 < x \leqslant 70$ is missing.

Calculate the frequency density for the missing bar.

b Calculate an estimate of the mean age of the passengers.

[Grade A]

8 A store conducted a survey into how far shoppers travel to the store.
They asked 200 shoppers.

The results are shown in the cumulative frequency diagram on the right.

Use the diagram to answer these questions.

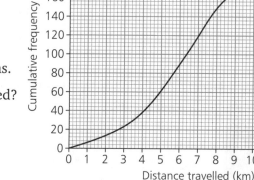

a What was the median distance travelled?

b What was the upper quartile?

c What percentage of those questioned travelled 10 km or more?

d **i** Copy and complete this frequency table:

Distance travelled, d (km)	$0 < d \leqslant 2$	$2 < d \leqslant 5$	$5 < d \leqslant 7$	$7 < d \leqslant 8$	$8 < d \leqslant 10$	$10 < d \leqslant 14$
Frequency						

ii Use the information in your table to draw a histogram. Use a scale of 1 cm to represent 1 km on the horizontal axis, and 1 cm to represent 5 on the vertical axis for frequency density.

[Grades B–A]

Constructions and matrices

Learning outcomes

After this chapter you should be able to:

- measure lines and angles　　　　　　　　　　　　　　　　　　　 `G` `F`
- construct triangles and other simple geometrical figures from given data, using rulers, protractors, compasses and set squares　　　　　　　　　　　　 `F`
- construct angle bisectors and perpendicular bisectors, using straight edges and a pair of compasses only　　　　　　　　　　　　　　　　　　 `C`
- read and make scale drawings　　　　　　　　　　　　　　 `E` `D` `C`
- use loci to find sets of points which are:
  - at a given distance from a given point and from a straight line　`C`
  - equidistant from two points and from two straight lines　　　`C`
- use vector notation to describe a movement　　　　　　　　　　 `C`
- add and subtract vectors, and multiply a vector by a scalar　　 `E` `D` `C`
- calculate the magnitude of a vector　　　　　　　　　　　　　 `C`
- use the sum and difference of two vectors to express given vectors in terms of two vectors, and use position vectors　　　　　　　　　　　　　 `A`
- display information in the form of a matrix of any order　　　　 `B`
- calculate the sum and product of two matrices, and the product of a matrix and a scalar quantity　　　　　　　　　　　　　　　　　　 `B` `A`
- use the algebra of 2 × 2 matrices including the zero and identity 2 × 2 matrices　`A`
- calculate the determinant and inverse of a matrix　　　　　　 `A` `A*`
- describe transformations using matrices.　　　　　　　　　　　 `A`

Revise 7.1 Constructions

Constructing triangles

Measuring and drawing angles

An **angle** is a measure of turn, or change in direction.

You measure angles with a protractor.

Protractors have two scales, one numbered clockwise and the other anticlockwise.

To measure an angle, place the cross at the centre of the protractor on the vertex of the angle.

Place one of the zero lines of the protractor on one of the lines making the angle.

This angle is 39°.

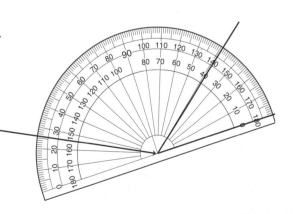

Constructing an SAS triangle

The angle between two given sides is called the **included angle**.

An SAS triangle is probably the easiest type of triangle to construct.

For example, to draw a triangle ABC with $AB = 6$ cm, $AC = 5$ cm, and angle $BAC = 43°$ the steps are:

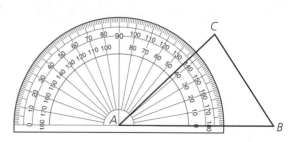

- draw the longer side (AB) 6 cm long

- then measure an angle of 43° at A

- extend this line to 5 cm to point C

- then draw BC to complete the triangle.

Constructing an SSS triangle

Use a pair of compasses to construct a triangle when you are given the length of three sides.

For example, to draw a triangle with sides of 7 cm, 6 cm and 4 cm, the steps are:

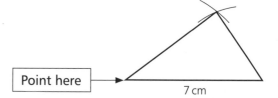

- draw the longest side first (7 cm)

- open the compasses to 6 cm

- put the point on one end of the line and draw an arc

- open the compasses to 4 cm

- put the point on the other end of the 7 cm line, and draw an arc to cross the first arc (as shown)

- finally, connect the two ends of the line to the intersection of the arcs.

Exam tip

Draw a sketch of the triangle and write the given measurements on it. This will help you to see how to construct your triangle.

Constructing an SSA triangle

If the angle you are given is not the included angle, there are two possible triangles.

If you are given the lengths of AB and AC and the size of angle B:

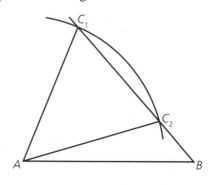

- draw AB, and measure the angle at B

- with compasses open to the length of AC and the point on A, draw an arc to cross the line from B

- the arc crosses at two points (labelled C_1 and C_2)

- then join either of these to A to give a triangle matching the description.

This is called the **ambiguous case**, which means there are two triangles that match the description.

Constructing an ASA triangle

If you know two angles of a triangle, you can calculate the third angle, as the sum of the angles is 180°.

For example, to construct a triangle ABC with $AB = 5$ cm, angle $BAC = 37°$ and angle $ACB = 100°$, the steps are:

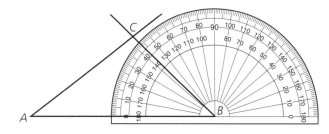

- draw the line AB, 5 cm long
- measure an angle of 37° at A
- the angle at $B = 180° - 37° - 100° = 43°$, as the angles in a triangle add up to 180°
- draw angle $ABC = 43°$, making the lines longer if necessary so they intersect at C.

Constructing parallel lines

Use a ruler and set square to construct parallel lines.

Place a set square on a straight line.

Put a ruler against the **hypotenuse** (long side) of the set square.

Hold the ruler in position and slide the set square along the ruler.

You can draw a line parallel to the first line.

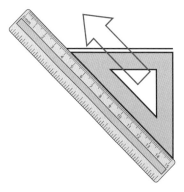

Bisectors and scale drawings

To **bisect** means to cut in half.

A **perpendicular bisector** cuts a line in half at right angles.

An **angle bisector** cuts an angle in half.

To construct a perpendicular bisector

The perpendicular bisector of a line AB joins all the points which are **equidistant** (the same distance) from A and B.

Open the compasses to more than half the length of AB.

Put the point on A and make two arcs, one on each side of the line.

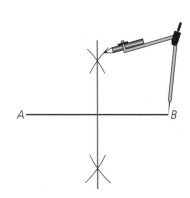

Now move the compass point to B and repeat. The arcs must cross the first two arcs.

Then draw a line passing through the two intersections.

This is the perpendicular bisector of AB.

To construct an angle bisector

The bisector of angle *BAC* joins all the points equidistant from *AB* and *AC*.

To bisect (or cut exactly in half) an angle *BAC*, put the compass point on the vertex, *A*, and make equal marks at *B* and *C* along each arm of the angle.

Using *B* and *C* as centres, draw two arcs to cross inside the angle, at *D*.

Draw the angle bisector from *A* through *D*.

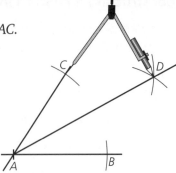

Scale drawings

A **scale drawing** is an accurate drawing that shows the exact shape but does not use the actual size.

The scale can be written in words, for example '1 cm represents 10 m'. | **Remember 1 m = 100 cm**

It can be written as a ratio, for example 1 : 1000.

Worked examples

Constructing a quadrilateral from given information

C

Construct a quadrilateral *ABCD* with *AB* = 8 cm, *BC* = 7 cm, *CD* = 9 cm, *AD* = 8 cm and angle *ABC* = 58°.

Solution

First draw a rough sketch:

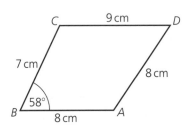

To make an accurate construction:

- draw *BA*, 8 cm long

- measure an angle of 58° at *B* and draw *BC* = 7 cm

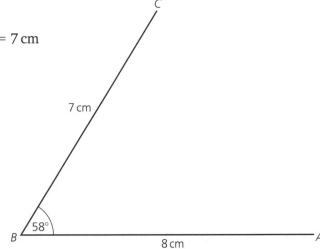

- then draw an 8 cm arc from *A* and a 9 cm arc from *C* to meet at *D*
- join *AC* and *CD*.

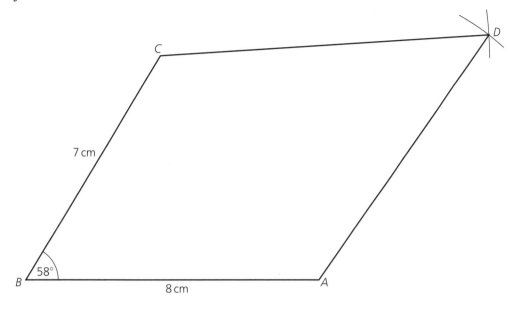

Constructing a scale drawing of a triangle

E

A triangular field *ABC* has sides of 100 m, 80 m and 75 m, as shown.

Use a scale of 1 cm to 10 m to make a scale drawing of the field.

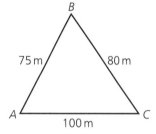

Solution

Draw *AC*, 10 cm long.

Open the compasses to 7.5 cm. Put the compass point on *A* and draw an arc.

Open the compasses to 8 cm. Put the compass point on *C* and draw an arc.

Label the point where the arcs cross as *B*.

Join *B* to *A* and *C*.

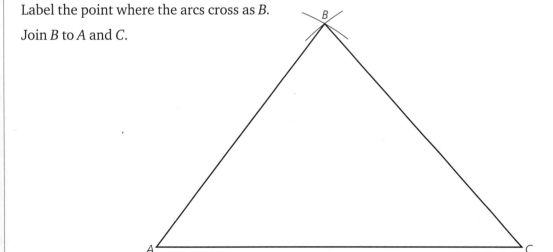

Revise 7.2 Loci

Constructing a locus

A **locus** is a path that follows a rule.

There are some standard constructions that deal with loci.

Points at a given distance from a fixed point

A **circle** is the locus of a point moving at a given distance from a fixed point.

Points at a given distance from a straight line

A point moving at a given distance from a straight line follows a line parallel to that line.

The locus consists of two parallel lines, one on either side of the original line.

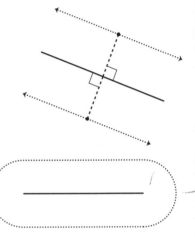

If the line ends (this is called a **line segment**), then the parallel lines are joined by semicircles.

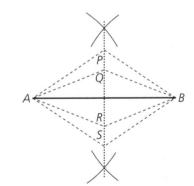

Points equidistant from two given points

All the points **equidistant** (the same distance) from A and B lie on the perpendicular bisector of AB.
This is shown by the dotted line.

P, Q, R and S are points that are equidistant from A and B.

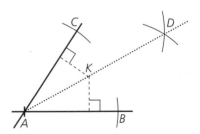

Points equidistant from two intersecting lines

All the points equidistant from two lines AB and AC lie on the bisector of angle BAC. This is shown by the dotted line AKD.

K is a point that is equidistant from AB and AC.

Loci and scale drawing

Many problems require the skills of constructions, loci and scale drawing.

Worked examples

Locus of a point around a square

[C]

Shade the area where points are less than 1 cm from the square.

Solution

Construct lines parallel to the sides of the square at a distance of 1 cm from the square.

Add quarter circles to the vertices of the outer square.

In the shaded area, points are less than 1 cm from the square.

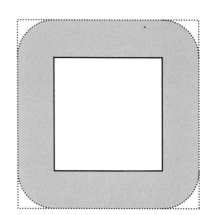

Loci using points and lines

[C]

a Draw the locus of points equidistant from *AB* and *AC*.

b Draw the locus of points equidistant from *A* and *C*.

c Draw the locus of points 3 cm from *A*.

d Shade the area within the acute angle *CAB* where points are closer to *AC* than to *AB*, closer to *C* than *A* and less than 3 cm from *A*.

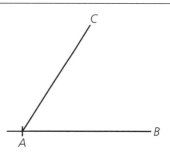

Solution

a This is the bisector of angle *BAC*.

b This is the perpendicular bisector of *AC*.

c This is a circle of radius 3 cm, centred on *A*.

d The required area is shaded in the diagram.

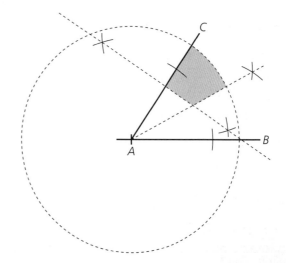

Loci and scale drawing

C

A garden *ABCD* is 28 m long and 16 m wide.

A building *AEFG* is 8 m long and 6 m wide.

A goat is tied to the point *G* on a rope 12 m long.

a Mark the area of the garden that the goat can reach.

b The owner wants to plant a tree so that it is equidistant from *D* and *E* but beyond the reach of the goat.

Mark the area where the tree can be planted.

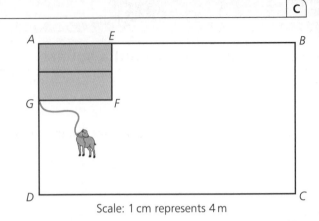

Scale: 1 cm represents 4 m

Solution

a The 12 m rope is represented by 3 cm.

Draw a quarter circle of radius 3 cm and centre *G*.

When the rope is pulled tight along *GF*, there is 4 m of rope beyond *F*.
This is represented by 1 cm.

Draw a quarter circle of radius 1 cm, with the centre at *F*.

The dotted area in the diagram is the area that the goat can reach.

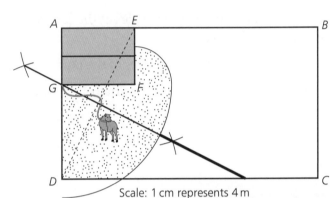

Scale: 1 cm represents 4 m

b For the tree to be equidistant from *D* and *E*, find the perpendicular bisector of *DE*.

The tree can be planted anywhere along the thick black line.

Exam tip

Leave your construction lines to show how you answered the question. Mark the answer region clearly.

Revise 7.3 Vectors

Combining vectors

Vector notation

A **vector** represents a movement.

It has a **magnitude** (or size) and a **direction**.

The movement from *A* to *B* can be written as $\vec{AB}$, or as **n**.

As a column vector, it is $\begin{pmatrix} 3 \\ -2 \end{pmatrix}$.

The top number represents a horizontal movement and the bottom number represents a vertical movement.

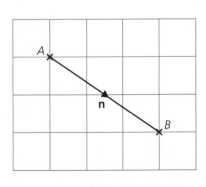

The column vector $\begin{pmatrix} 3 \\ -2 \end{pmatrix}$ means:

> move 3 units to the right (a negative number would indicate left), and
>
> move 2 units down (because the number is negative it means a downward movement).

So 3 is the horizontal component and -2 is the vertical component.

The vector going in the opposite direction is $\overrightarrow{BA} = -\mathbf{n} = \begin{pmatrix} -3 \\ 2 \end{pmatrix}$.

Adding and subtracting vectors

You add vectors by adding the horizontal components and the vertical components separately.

In vector terms, moving from A to B and then from B to C is identical to moving directly from A to C.

$$\overrightarrow{AB} + \overrightarrow{BC} = \begin{pmatrix} 5 \\ -2 \end{pmatrix} + \begin{pmatrix} -3 \\ -4 \end{pmatrix}$$
$$= \begin{pmatrix} 2 \\ -6 \end{pmatrix}$$
$$= \overrightarrow{AC}$$

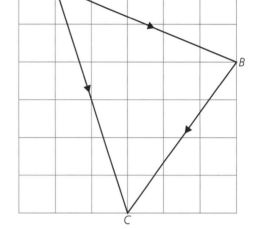

You subtract vectors by subtracting the horizontal components and the vertical components separately.

$$\overrightarrow{AC} - \overrightarrow{BC} = \begin{pmatrix} 2 \\ -6 \end{pmatrix} - \begin{pmatrix} -3 \\ -4 \end{pmatrix}$$
$$= \begin{pmatrix} 5 \\ -2 \end{pmatrix}$$
$$= \overrightarrow{AB}$$

Multiplying a vector by a scalar

Two vectors cannot be multiplied together.

You can multiply a vector by a **scalar** (a single number).

The vector $2\mathbf{a} = \mathbf{a} + \mathbf{a}$.

To multiply a vector by a scalar, multiply each component of the vector by the scalar:

$$4\begin{pmatrix} 2 \\ -3 \end{pmatrix} = \begin{pmatrix} 4 \times 2 \\ 4 \times -3 \end{pmatrix} = \begin{pmatrix} 8 \\ -12 \end{pmatrix}$$

> ### Exam tip
>
> A minus sign in front of a vector reverses the direction of movement. So $-\overrightarrow{BC} = \overrightarrow{CB}$.

The resultant vector is four times longer than the original vector, and goes in the same direction, so is parallel to the original vector.

If a vector is a multiple of another vector, then the two vectors are parallel.

The magnitude of a vector

The **magnitude**, or size, of a vector can be calculated using Pythagoras' theorem.

The vector $\begin{pmatrix} x \\ y \end{pmatrix}$ has a horizontal component of length x and a vertical component of length y.

The length of the vector is given by $l = \sqrt{x^2 + y^2}$.

The vector $\overrightarrow{AB} = \begin{pmatrix} 3 \\ -2 \end{pmatrix}$ has magnitude $\sqrt{3^2 + (-2)^2} = \sqrt{13}$ (or 3.6 to 1 d.p.).

The magnitude of a vector $\mathbf{a}$ is written $|\mathbf{a}|$.

So $|\mathbf{a}| = \sqrt{13}$ (or 3.6 to 1 d.p.).

Vector geometry

Position vectors

On a coordinate grid, the point $(0, 0)$ is usually marked as O, and is called the **origin**.

A **position vector** gives the vector from the origin to a point.

The movement from the origin to a point $A(-1, 2)$ is $\overrightarrow{OA} = \begin{pmatrix} -1 \\ 2 \end{pmatrix}$

This is called the position vector of A.

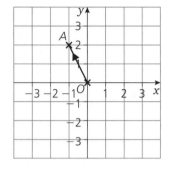

Collinear points

Collinear points lie on a straight line.

If A, B and C are collinear, then AB and AC will be parallel, so $\overrightarrow{AC}$ will be a multiple of $\overrightarrow{AB}$.

Worked example

Vector geometry

A

$OABC$ is a parallelogram.

The position vectors of A and C are **a** and **c**.

X lies on AC so that $AX = \frac{1}{3}AC$.

Y is the midpoint of AB.

Show that OXY is a straight line.

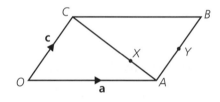

Solution

$\overrightarrow{OX} = \overrightarrow{OA} + \overrightarrow{AX}$

$\quad = OA + \frac{1}{3}AC$

$\quad = \mathbf{a} + \frac{1}{3}(\mathbf{c} - \mathbf{a})$

$\quad = \frac{2}{3}\mathbf{a} + \frac{1}{3}\mathbf{c}$

$\quad = \frac{1}{3}(2\mathbf{a} + \mathbf{c})$

$\overrightarrow{OY} = \overrightarrow{OA} + \overrightarrow{AY}$

$\quad = \overrightarrow{OA} + \frac{1}{2}\overrightarrow{AB}$

$\quad = \mathbf{a} + \frac{1}{2}\mathbf{c} \qquad (\text{as } \overrightarrow{AB} = \overrightarrow{OC})$

$\quad = \frac{1}{2}(2\mathbf{a} + \mathbf{c})$

$\overrightarrow{OX}$ and $\overrightarrow{OY}$ are both multiples of $(2\mathbf{a} + \mathbf{c})$, so are parallel.

But they both pass through O, so O, X and Y are collinear.

Revise 7.4 Matrices

Matrix calculations

A **matrix** is a rectangular set of numbers.

Matrices are usually identified with a capital letter.

Matrix addition and subtraction

The matrix $\begin{pmatrix} 1 & 2 & 0 \\ -2 & 3 & 1 \end{pmatrix}$ has two rows and three columns. The order of the matrix is 2×3.

> You can only add or subtract matrices that are of the same order (have the same number of rows and the same number of columns).

You add or subtract the numbers that are in the same position:

$$\begin{pmatrix} 1 & 3 \\ -2 & 4 \\ 3 & -1 \end{pmatrix} - \begin{pmatrix} 2 & 1 \\ 3 & -2 \\ 2 & -4 \end{pmatrix} = \begin{pmatrix} 1-2 & 3--1 \\ -2-3 & 4--2 \\ 3-2 & -1--4 \end{pmatrix} = \begin{pmatrix} -1 & 2 \\ -5 & 6 \\ 1 & 3 \end{pmatrix}$$

Multiplying a matrix by a scalar

A **scalar** is a single number.

To multiply a matrix by a scalar, each number in the matrix is multiplied by the scalar.

$$4 \times \begin{pmatrix} 1 & 3 \\ -2 & 2 \end{pmatrix} = \begin{pmatrix} 4 \times 1 & 4 \times 3 \\ 4 \times -2 & 4 \times 2 \end{pmatrix} = \begin{pmatrix} 4 & 12 \\ -8 & 8 \end{pmatrix}$$

Multiplying two matrices

You can only multiply two matrices if the number of columns of the first matrix is equal to the number of rows of the second matrix.

The answer has the same number of rows as the first matrix and the same number of columns as the second matrix.

To multiply matrices, the numbers in a *row* of the first matrix are multiplied by the numbers in a *column* of the second matrix. The results are added together.

$$\begin{pmatrix} 1 & 3 & 0 \\ -2 & 2 & -1 \end{pmatrix} \begin{pmatrix} -3 & 1 \\ 2 & 5 \\ -4 & 6 \end{pmatrix} = \begin{pmatrix} \text{first row} \times \text{first column} & \text{first row} \times \text{second column} \\ \text{second row} \times \text{first column} & \text{second row} \times \text{second column} \end{pmatrix}$$

$$= \begin{pmatrix} 1 \times -3 + 3 \times 2 + 0 \times -4 & 1 \times 1 + 3 \times 5 + 0 \times 6 \\ -2 \times -3 + 2 \times 2 + -1 \times -4 & -2 \times 1 + 2 \times 5 + -1 \times 6 \end{pmatrix}$$

$$= \begin{pmatrix} -3 + 6 + 0 & 1 + 15 + 0 \\ 6 + 4 + 4 & -2 + 10 + -6 \end{pmatrix} = \begin{pmatrix} 3 & 16 \\ 14 & 2 \end{pmatrix}$$

Matrix algebra

The **zero matrix** is the matrix which does not produce any change when added to or subtracted from another matrix.

The zero matrix for a matrix **A** is the same order as **A** and every number is 0.

For example, $\begin{pmatrix} 2 & -1 & 3 \\ 4 & 0 & -5 \end{pmatrix} + \begin{pmatrix} 0 & 0 & 0 \\ 0 & 0 & 0 \end{pmatrix} = \begin{pmatrix} 2 & -1 & 3 \\ 4 & 0 & -5 \end{pmatrix}.$

The **identity matrix**, **I**, is the matrix which does not produce any change when multiplied with another matrix. It is a square matrix. The numbers in the diagonal from top left to bottom right are all 1. The rest of the numbers are 0.

For example, $\begin{pmatrix} 2 & 4 \\ -1 & -3 \\ 0 & 5 \end{pmatrix} \begin{pmatrix} 1 & 0 \\ 0 & 1 \end{pmatrix} = \begin{pmatrix} 2 & 4 \\ -1 & -3 \\ 0 & 5 \end{pmatrix}$

The **inverse matrix** of M is written as M^{-1}.

This is the matrix such that $M \times M^{-1} =$ the identity matrix.

For the matrix $\begin{pmatrix} a & b \\ c & d \end{pmatrix}$, the inverse matrix is $\dfrac{1}{ad - bc} \begin{pmatrix} d & -b \\ -c & a \end{pmatrix}$.

$ad - bc$ is called the **determinant** of the matrix.

> **Exam tip**
>
> In matrix algebra, **AB** is not the same as **BA**.
>
> There is one exception to this rule: if one of the matrices is the identity matrix then **AI** = **IA**.

Matrices and transformations

Translations

You can use a vector to describe a translation.

You can find the image of $P(4, 2)$ when it is translated by vector $\begin{pmatrix} 2 \\ -3 \end{pmatrix}$ by adding vectors. Add the translation vector to the position vector of P:

$$\begin{pmatrix} 4 \\ 2 \end{pmatrix} + \begin{pmatrix} 2 \\ -3 \end{pmatrix} = \begin{pmatrix} 6 \\ -1 \end{pmatrix}$$

The image of P is the point $P_1(6, -1)$.

Other transformations

To produce a transformation with a matrix, pre-multiply by the transformation matrix (put the transformation matrix first).

Shears

A matrix of the form $\begin{pmatrix} 1 & k \\ 0 & 1 \end{pmatrix}$ produces a shear parallel to the x-axis.

For example, the matrix $\begin{pmatrix} 1 & 2 \\ 0 & 1 \end{pmatrix}$ transforms the triangle

with vertices at (2, 1), (3, 1) and (2, 4) to

$\begin{pmatrix} 1 & 2 \\ 0 & 1 \end{pmatrix}\begin{pmatrix} 2 & 3 & 2 \\ 1 & 1 & 4 \end{pmatrix} = \begin{pmatrix} 4 & 5 & 10 \\ 1 & 1 & 4 \end{pmatrix}$, a triangle with vertices

at (4, 1), (5, 1) and (10, 4).

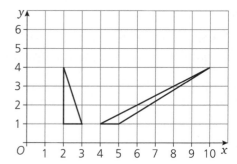

Reflections

Reflections are produced by multiplying by certain matrices.

The matrix $\begin{pmatrix} 1 & 0 \\ 0 & -1 \end{pmatrix}$ produces a reflection in the x-axis.

The matrix $\begin{pmatrix} -1 & 0 \\ 0 & 1 \end{pmatrix}$ produces a reflection in the y-axis.

The matrix $\begin{pmatrix} 0 & 1 \\ 1 & 0 \end{pmatrix}$ produces a reflection in the line $y = x$.

The matrix $\begin{pmatrix} 0 & -1 \\ -1 & 0 \end{pmatrix}$ produces a reflection in the line $y = -x$.

Rotations

Rotations are also produced by multiplication.

The matrix $\begin{pmatrix} 0 & 1 \\ -1 & 0 \end{pmatrix}$ produces a 90° clockwise rotation about the origin.

The matrix $\begin{pmatrix} 0 & -1 \\ 1 & 0 \end{pmatrix}$ produces a 90° anticlockwise rotation about the origin.

Inverses

A transformation matrix **M** transforms a shape S into S'.

The inverse matrix, $\mathbf{M}^{-1}$, transforms S' into S.

For example, the inverse matrix of a 90° clockwise rotation, $\begin{pmatrix} 0 & 1 \\ -1 & 0 \end{pmatrix}$,

is a 90° anticlockwise rotation matrix, $\begin{pmatrix} 0 & -1 \\ 1 & 0 \end{pmatrix}$.

Enlargements

Multiplication by the matrix $\begin{pmatrix} n & 0 \\ 0 & n \end{pmatrix}$ produces an enlargement, scale factor n, centre the origin.

Combinations of transformations

To produce two transformations P followed by Q on **M**, calculate $Q(P\mathbf{M})$.

$Q(P\mathbf{M}) = (QP)\mathbf{M}$, so QP gives a single matrix that produces the single transformation to replace P and Q.

Exam tip

When combining matrices for two transformations, you pre-multiply, so the first transformation is on the right of the second.

Worked examples

Matrix algebra

$\mathbf{A} = \begin{pmatrix} 4 & 5 \\ 2 & 3 \end{pmatrix}$ and $\mathbf{B} = \begin{pmatrix} 8 & 11 \\ 4 & 7 \end{pmatrix}$

If $\mathbf{AC} = \mathbf{B}$, find **C**.

Solution

If $\mathbf{C} = \begin{pmatrix} a & b \\ c & d \end{pmatrix}$, then

$\begin{pmatrix} 4 & 5 \\ 2 & 3 \end{pmatrix} \times \begin{pmatrix} a & b \\ c & d \end{pmatrix} = \begin{pmatrix} 8 & 11 \\ 4 & 7 \end{pmatrix}$

The determinant of $\mathbf{A} = 4 \times 3 - 5 \times 2 = 12 - 10 = 2$.

So $\mathbf{A}^{-1} = \frac{1}{2}\begin{pmatrix} 3 & -5 \\ -2 & 4 \end{pmatrix}$

Pre-multiplying both sides by $\mathbf{A}^{-1}$ gives

$\frac{1}{2}\begin{pmatrix} 3 & -5 \\ -2 & 4 \end{pmatrix} \times \begin{pmatrix} 4 & 5 \\ 2 & 3 \end{pmatrix} \times \begin{pmatrix} a & b \\ c & d \end{pmatrix} = \frac{1}{2}\begin{pmatrix} 3 & -5 \\ -2 & 4 \end{pmatrix} \times \begin{pmatrix} 8 & 11 \\ 4 & 7 \end{pmatrix}$

$\begin{pmatrix} 1 & 0 \\ 0 & 1 \end{pmatrix} \times \begin{pmatrix} a & b \\ c & d \end{pmatrix} = \begin{pmatrix} 2 & -1 \\ 0 & 3 \end{pmatrix}$

$\begin{pmatrix} a & b \\ c & d \end{pmatrix} = \begin{pmatrix} 2 & -1 \\ 0 & 3 \end{pmatrix} = \mathbf{C}$

Matrix transformations

The transformation B maps the rectangle $E(1, 1)$, $F(3, 1)$, $G(3, 2)$, $H(1, 2)$ to $E'(2, 2)$, $F'(6, 4)$, $G'(6, 5)$, $H'(2, 3)$.

a Find the 2×2 matrix **B**, which represents the transformation B.

b The point P has coordinates $(3, -1)$.

  Find the coordinates of $B(P)$.

c Find $\mathbf{B}^{-1}$, the inverse of the matrix **B**.

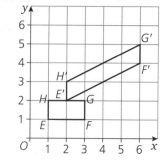

Solution

a If $\mathbf{B} = \begin{pmatrix} a & b \\ c & d \end{pmatrix}$, then

$$\begin{pmatrix} a & b \\ c & d \end{pmatrix} \times \begin{pmatrix} 1 & 3 & 3 & 1 \\ 1 & 1 & 2 & 2 \end{pmatrix} = \begin{pmatrix} 2 & 6 & 6 & 2 \\ 2 & 4 & 5 & 3 \end{pmatrix}$$

$$\begin{pmatrix} a+b & 3a+b & 3a+2b & a+2b \\ c+d & 3c+d & 3c+2d & c+2d \end{pmatrix} = \begin{pmatrix} 2 & 6 & 6 & 2 \\ 2 & 4 & 5 & 3 \end{pmatrix}$$

This gives you eight possible simultaneous equations:

$a + b = 2$ $\qquad c + d = 2$

$3a + b = 6$ $\qquad c + 2d = 3$

$2a = 4$ $\qquad\qquad d = 1, c = 1$

$a = 2, b = 0$

$\mathbf{B} = \begin{pmatrix} 2 & 0 \\ 1 & 1 \end{pmatrix}$

b $\mathbf{B}(P)$ is given by $\begin{pmatrix} 2 & 0 \\ 1 & 1 \end{pmatrix}\begin{pmatrix} 3 \\ -1 \end{pmatrix} = \begin{pmatrix} 6 \\ 2 \end{pmatrix}$

The coordinates of $\mathbf{B}(P)$ are $(6, 2)$.

c The determinant of $\begin{pmatrix} 2 & 0 \\ 1 & 1 \end{pmatrix} = 2 \times 1 - 0 \times 1 = 2$

$\mathbf{B}^{-1} = \dfrac{1}{2}\begin{pmatrix} 1 & 0 \\ -1 & 2 \end{pmatrix}$

Exam tip

- A full description of a reflection includes the line of symmetry.
- A full description of a rotation includes the centre of rotation, the angle of rotation and the direction.
- A full description of a translation includes the vector.
- A full description of an enlargement includes the centre of enlargement and the scale factor.
- A full description of a shear includes the invariant line and the image of one point that is not on the invariant line.

Practise 7.1 – 7.4

1 The diagram shows a sketch of a semicircle with a radius of 7 cm. AB is a diameter and O is the centre.

C is a point on the semicircle so that angle $BAC = 30°$.

a Make an accurate drawing of the semicircle and the line AC.

b **i** Construct the perpendicular bisector of AC.

  ii What do you notice about the line you have drawn?

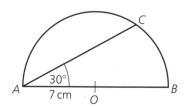

[Grades D–C]

2 *A*, *B* and *C* are three towns.

The distances between them are shown on the sketch map.

a Make an accurate drawing of the towns, using a scale of 1 cm to 2 km.

b A store, *S*, is on the line *AB*, equidistant from *A* and *B*.

Construct the perpendicular bisector of *AB* to find the position of the store.

c Use your drawing to find the distance from *C* to the store.

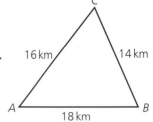

[Grades E–C]

3 **a** Construct a triangle *ABC* with *AB* = 11 cm, *AC* = 9 cm and *BC* = 7 cm.

b Construct the bisector of angle *ABC*. Label the point *D* where it crosses *AC*.

c Construct the perpendicular bisector of *CD*.

[Grades E–C]

4

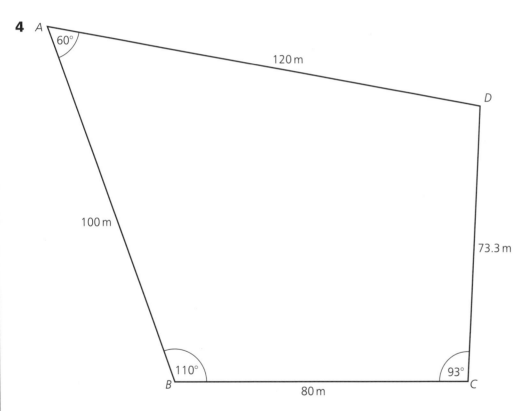

The diagram is a scale drawing of a field. The actual length of the side *AB* is 100 metres.

a Write the scale of the drawing in the form 1 : *n*, where *n* is an integer.

In part **b** use a straight edge and compasses only. Leave in your construction lines.

b **i** Make a copy of the scale drawing.

ii A tree in the field is equidistant from *A* and *D*. Construct the line on which the tree stands.

iii The tree is also equidistant from the sides *BC* and *AB*. Mark the position of the tree with the letter *T*.

[Grades D–C]

5 The diagram shows a sketch of an island.

A and *B* are two radio masts, 120 km apart.

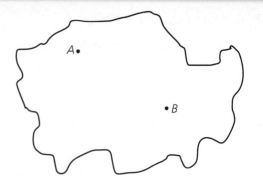

a Using a scale of 1 cm to 20 km, make a sketch of the island, marking *A* and *B*, 120 km apart.

b The mast at *A* has a range of 60 km.

The mast at *B* has a range of 80 km.

Shade on your map the area of the island within range of at least one mast.

[Grades E–C]

6 Four roads, *AB*, *BC*, *CD* and *AD* make a rhombus with sides of 220 m.

Angle *ABC* = 80°.

a Using a scale of 1 cm to represent 20 m, make an accurate scale drawing of the roads.

b A man wants to build a house in the land between the roads.

He must build the house so that:

i it is at least 30 m away from the roads

ii it is closer to *B* than *A*

iii it is closer to *AD* than *AB*.

Shade the area where the house can be built.

[Grades D–C]

7 $\mathbf{a} = \begin{pmatrix} 3 \\ -1 \end{pmatrix}$ and $\mathbf{b} = \begin{pmatrix} -2 \\ 1 \end{pmatrix}$.

Work out:

a $\mathbf{a} + \mathbf{b}$ **b** $\mathbf{b} - \mathbf{a}$ **c** $2\mathbf{a} - \mathbf{b}$ **d** $|2\mathbf{a} - \mathbf{b}|$.

[Grade E]

8 In the diagram, $\overrightarrow{DA} = \mathbf{a}$, $\overrightarrow{AB} = 3\mathbf{a} + 2\mathbf{b}$, $\overrightarrow{CB} = \mathbf{a} + \mathbf{b}$, and $\overrightarrow{DC} = 3\mathbf{a} + \mathbf{b}$.

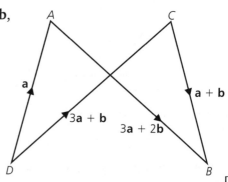

a Find, in terms of **a** and **b**:

i $\overrightarrow{AC}$

ii $\overrightarrow{DB}$.

b Show that *ACBD* is a trapezium.

[Grade B]

9 a Multiply $\begin{pmatrix} 2 & 3 \\ 1 & -4 \\ -2 & 0 \end{pmatrix} \begin{pmatrix} 3 & -1 \\ 5 & -1 \end{pmatrix}$.

b Find the inverse of $\begin{pmatrix} 3 & -1 \\ 5 & -1 \end{pmatrix}$.

[Grade A]

10 $A = \begin{pmatrix} 2 \\ -3 \end{pmatrix}$, $B = \begin{pmatrix} -2 & -2 \\ 2 & 3 \end{pmatrix}$, $C = \begin{pmatrix} 3 & -2 \\ 5 & -3 \end{pmatrix}$.

    a Which of these multiplications *cannot* be carried out?

       i BA   **ii** BC   **iii** AB   **iv** CA

    b Show that $(\mathbf{BC})^{-1} = \mathbf{C}^{-1}\mathbf{B}^{-1}$.

[Grade A]

11

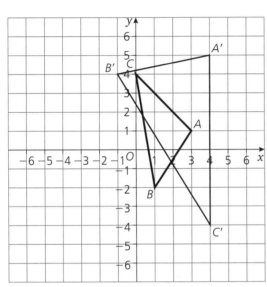

A 2×2 transformation matrix **M** maps triangle $A(3, 1)$, $B(1, -2)$, $C(0, 4)$ to $A'(4, 5)$, $B'(-1, 4)$, $C'(4, -4)$.

    a Find the matrix **M**.

    b Find $\mathbf{M}^{-1}$.

[Grade A*]

8 Graphs

Learning outcomes

After this chapter you should be able to:

- use Cartesian coordinates to plot points on a graph | G | F |
- draw and interpret real-life graphs such as a conversion graph or a travel graph | F | E | D |
- find rates of change in distance–time and speed–time graphs | C | B |
- calculate distance travelled as the area under a linear speed–time graph | B |
- draw a straight line graph from given data | E | D |
- find the gradient and the equation of a given straight line | C |
- find the equation of a line parallel to a given straight line | C |
- find the coordinates of the midpoint of a line segment | C |
- draw and interpret the graph of a quadratic function or a cubic function | E | D | C |
- draw the graph of reciprocal and exponential functions | C | B | A |
- estimate gradients of curves by drawing tangents | B |
- solve equations approximately by graphical methods. | C | B | A |

Revise 8.1 Real-life graphs

Plotting points

Cartesian coordinates use two **axes** at right angles.

A point on the grid is described by two coordinates.

The point where the axes cross is called the **origin**, which is the point (0, 0).

The **x-coordinate** measures **horizontal** distance from the origin.

The **y-coordinate** measures **vertical** distance from the origin.

Conversion graphs

To draw a **conversion graph**, you need to know two equivalent measurements.

For example: a distance of 5 miles is equivalent to 8 kilometres.

We also know that 0 miles is the same as 0 kilometres.

These equivalent measurements are used in the first worked example.

Exam tip

The scales on the two axes may not be the same. Read off values very carefully.

Distance–time graphs

This distance–time graph shows a two-hour bus journey.

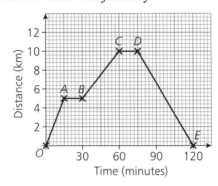

Time is always shown on the horizontal axis and distance on the vertical axis.

On this graph, the time is shown in minutes from the start of the journey.

Horizontal parts of the graph (*AB* and *CD*) show when the bus has stopped.

The bus travels for 15 minutes, (*OA*), stops for 15 minutes and then travels on for 30 minutes (*BC*).

It reaches its destination, 10 km from the start, after one hour.

The section *CD* shows that the bus stays at its destination for 15 minutes.

The section *DE* shows the return journey, which takes 45 minutes.

Speed–time graphs

On a speed–time graph, time is shown on the horizontal axis and speed is shown on the vertical axis.

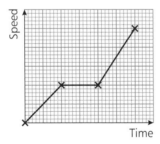

From a speed–time graph you can work out **acceleration**, using the formula:

$$\text{Acceleration} = \frac{\text{increase in speed}}{\text{time}}$$

If the speed is decreasing, use the formula:

$$\text{Deceleration} = \frac{\text{decrease in speed}}{\text{time}}$$

A speed–time graph can also be used to find the distance travelled.

$$\textbf{Distance travelled = area under the graph}$$

Exam tip

On a speed–time graph, the gradient tells you the acceleration. If part of the graph has a zero gradient, this shows that the bus has no acceleration, NOT that it has stopped moving.

Worked examples

Conversion graph   E

5 miles = 8 kilometres.

a Draw a graph to convert miles to kilometres.

b Use your graph to change 3 miles to kilometres.

b Change 12 miles to kilometres.

Solution

a Label axes from 0 to 5 miles horizontally and from 0 to 8 km vertically.

   The points (0, 0) and (5, 8) lie on the graph so plot these and join them with a ruled line.

b Start at 3 miles. Draw a vertical line up to meet the graph (at *P*).

   Draw a horizontal line across from P to the vertical axis and read off the value there.

   3 miles = 4.8 km

c 12 miles = 4 × 3 miles

   = 4 × 4.8 km

   = 19.2 km

> Label the axes to make it clear which shows miles and which shows kilometres.

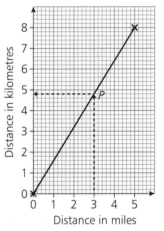

Distance–time graph   E D C

The graph shows Paul's car journey from home to work.

a What happens between 0910 and 0915?

b What is Paul's average speed from *Q* to *R*?

c How does the graph show that the average speed from *O* to *P* is greater than the average speed from *Q* to *R*?

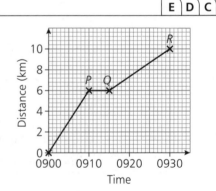

Solution

a Between 0910 and 0915 *(PQ)* Paul is at a standstill.

b Between *Q* and *R* the distance travelled is 4 km and the time is 15 minutes.

   4 km in 15 minutes = 16 km in 60 minutes

   The average speed is 16 km/h.

c The gradient is steeper from *O* to *P* than from *Q* to *R*.

Speed–time graph

B A

This speed–time graph shows a bus journey.

a Work out the acceleration of the bus over the first 10 minutes.

b What happens between 1110 and 1115?

c Calculate the total distance travelled on this journey.

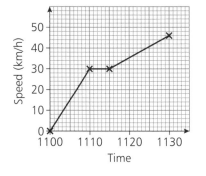

Solution

a In the first 10 minutes, the speed of the bus goes from 0 to 30 km/h.

10 minutes is one-sixth of an hour. | You need to work in hours because the speed is in km/h.

Acceleration = $30 \div \frac{1}{6} = 180 \, \text{km/h}^2$

b The bus travels at a steady speed of 30 km/h.

c Divide up the area under the graph as shown below.

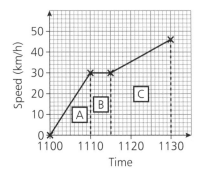

Area A = $\frac{1}{2}\left(\frac{1}{6} \times 30\right) = 2.5 \, \text{km}$

Area B = $\frac{1}{12} \times 30 = 2.5 \, \text{km}$

Area C = $\frac{1}{2}(30 + 46) \times \frac{1}{4} = 9.5 \, \text{km}$

Total distance travelled = 14.5 km.

Revise 8.2 Straight line graphs

Drawing a straight line graph

An equation such as $y = 4x + 5$ can be shown on a graph.

The graph will be a straight line and $y = 4x + 5$ is called a **linear equation**.

To draw the graph, work out the coordinates of three points on the line.

> **Take $x = 0$ as one of the values because it is easy to substitute in the equation.**

Exam tip

The third point is a check to make sure your working is correct.

If your three points are not in a straight line, go back and check your working.

Gradients of straight line graphs

The **gradient** is a measure of how steep the line is.

$$\text{Gradient} = \frac{\text{change in vertical distance}}{\text{change in horizontal distance}} = \frac{y}{x}$$

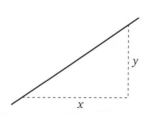

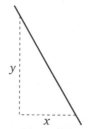

This line has a positive gradient.   This line has a negative gradient.

You can work out the gradient from the graph, using right-angled triangles as shown above.

You can also find the gradient from the equation of the line.

Write the equation in the form $y = mx + c$.

x and y are the **variables** in the equation (because they can take different values).

The number in front of x, 'm', is the **coefficient** of x and is the gradient of the line.

When $x = 0$, $y = c$, so this is where the line crosses the y-axis.

For example, the gradient of the line $y = -4x + 5$ is -4 and it crosses the y-axis at $(0, 5)$.

Finding the equation of a straight line graph

First find the gradient, m.

Then try to find c by looking to see where the line crosses the y-axis.

Or you can substitute a pair of coordinates to find c.

Parallel lines

Parallel lines have the same gradient.

Any line parallel to $y = 5x - 3$, will be $y = 5x + c$.

If the line goes through, for example, $(2, 3)$, substitute these values to find c.

$$3 = 5 \times 2 + c$$
$$3 = 10 + c$$
$$c = -7$$

so the line is $y = 5x - 7$.

Line segments

A **line segment** is the part of a line joining two points.

To find the midpoint of a line segment, find the mean of the coordinates of the end points.

Worked examples

A straight line graph

D

Draw the graph of $y = 7 - 2x$ for values of x from -1 to 5.

Solution

Choose three values of x and make a table of values.

Use the end values, -1 and 5, and 0 because it is easy to substitute.

x	-1	0	5
y	9	7	-3

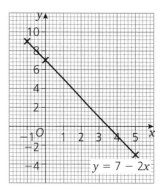

The gradient and equation of a given straight line

C

a Find the gradient of the line shown below.

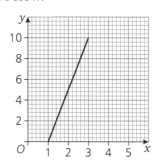

b Find the equation of the line.

Solution

a The gradient of this line is $\dfrac{10 - 0}{3 - 1} = 5$. ◄——— Using the largest possible triangle.

b Its equation is $y = 5x + c$ and it goes through $(1, 0)$.

$$0 = 5 + c$$ ◄——— Substitute the values $(1, 0)$ in the equation.

$$c = -5$$

The equation of the line is $y = 5x - 5$.

The equation of a line

C

A is the point $(-4, 2)$ and B is the point $(5, -1)$.

a Find the coordinates of the midpoint of the line segment AB.

b Find the equation of the line AB.

c Find the equation of a line parallel to AB, through the point $(1, 3)$.

Solution

Draw a sketch to show the positions of A and B.

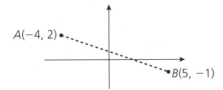

$A(-4, 2)$

$B(5, -1)$

a The midpoint is at $\left(\dfrac{-4 + 5}{2}, \dfrac{2 + -1}{2}\right) = (0.5, 0.5)$

b The gradient of AB is $\dfrac{2 - -1}{-4 - 5} = \dfrac{3}{-9} = -\dfrac{1}{3}$

The equation of AB is $y = -\dfrac{1}{3}x + c$.

When $x = -4, y = 2$, so substitute these numbers in the equation.

$2 = -\dfrac{-4}{3} + c$

$6 = 4 + 3c$ ◄————————————————————— | Multiply throughout by **3**.

$c = \dfrac{2}{3}$

The equation of AB is $y = -\dfrac{1}{3}x + \dfrac{2}{3}$, which can also be written as $3y + x = 2$.

c Any parallel line will have an equation $3y + x = c$

When $x = 1, y = 3$ so $3y + x = 3 \times 3 + 1 = 10$.

The parallel line is $3y + x = 10$.

Revise 8.3 Graphs of functions

All the graphs in this section are curves, so you have to plot more than three points in order to draw them. Your table of values should include all the integer values of x in the given range.

Quadratic functions

Every **quadratic function** contains a term in x^2 but no higher powers of x such as x^3 or x^4.

$f(x) = 3x^2 - 3x - 2$ is a quadratic function but $g(x) = 3x^2 + x^3$ is not.

To work out values of y for an expression such as $y = 3x^2 - 3x - 2$, put some extra lines into your table:

x	-2	-1	0	1	2	3	4
$3x^2$	12	3	0	3	12	27	48
$-3x$	$+6$	$+3$	0	-3	-6	-9	-12
y	16	4	-2	-2	4	16	34

Add the values in the middle two lines together and then subtract 2, to get the values of y.

Plot the points and join them with a smooth curve.

Quadratic expressions with (+) x^2 have this shape:

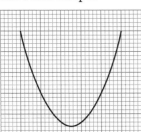

Quadratic expressions with $-x^2$ have this shape:

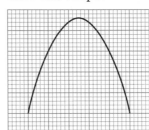

Exam tip

If you join your plotted points with straight lines, you will lose marks.

Cubic functions

$f(x) = x^3 + x - 2$ is an example of a **cubic function**.

Every cubic function contains a term in x^3.

Cubic expressions with (+) x^3 have this shape:

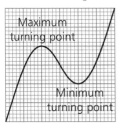

Cubic expressions with $-x^3$ have this shape:

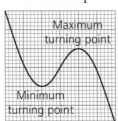

Some cubic functions have their two turning points together and look like one of these:

Exponential functions

$f(x) = 3^x$ is an exponential function.

The base, 3, is a constant and the power, x, is a variable.

When $x = 0$, $f(x) = 1$, so the graph goes through (0, 1).

When x is negative, $f(x)$ is less than 1 and when x takes positive values it becomes very large.

An exponential graph has this shape.

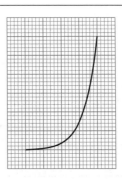

Graphs of reciprocal functions

The **reciprocal function** of x is $\frac{1}{x}$.

These are also reciprocal functions: $y = \frac{1}{x}$, $y = \frac{-2}{x}$, $y = \frac{50}{x}$.

This is the graph of $y = \frac{1}{x}$.

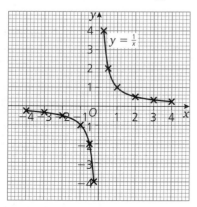

Exam tip

- Plot some points where x lies between 0 and 1 to help you to draw the right-hand part of the curve.

- Plot some points where x lies between -1 and 0 to help you to draw the left-hand part of the curve.

For reciprocal functions, when $x = 0$ the value of y cannot be found.

There is a break in the graph and it is said to be **discontinuous**.

Drawing a tangent to a curve

AB is a tangent to the curve at P.

Use a ruler to draw a tangent.

Your line must touch the curve but not cross it.

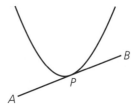

Estimating the gradient of a curve

To find the gradient of a curve at a given point, draw the tangent at the point and find its gradient.

This is the graph of $y = x^2$.

The tangent to the graph at $x = -1$ has been drawn.

The gradient is $\dfrac{5 - 1}{-3 - -1} = -2$.

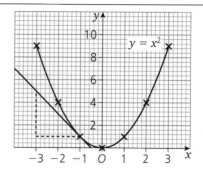

Solving equations by graphical methods

To solve the equation $f(x) = 0$, find where the graph of $y = f(x)$ crosses the line $y = 0$ (the x-axis).

To solve the equation $f(x) = g(x)$, draw $y = f(x)$ and $y = g(x)$ on the same grid.

The point where the two graphs meet is called the **intersection** of the graphs.

(There may be more than one intersection.)

The x-coordinate at the intersection is a solution of the equation $f(x) = g(x)$.

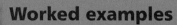

Worked examples

Graph of a cubic function

C

a Copy and complete the table of values for $f(x) = 6x - x^3$.

	−3	−2	−1	0	1	2	3
$6x$	−18	−12					18
$-x^3$	+27	+8					−27
	9	−4					−9

b Draw the graph of $y = f(x)$ for values of x from −3 to 3.

c Write down the coordinates of the maximum turning point on your graph.

d Use your graph to find approximate solutions of the equation $f(x) = 0$.

Solution

a To find y, add the two middle lines together.

	−3	−2	−1	0	1	2	3
$6x$	−18	−12	−6	0	6	12	18
$-x^3$	+27	+8	+1	0	−1	−8	−27
	9	−4	−5	0	5	4	−9

b

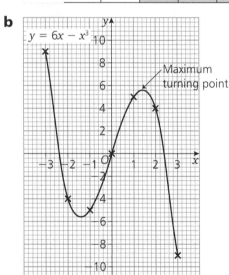

c The maximum turning point is at (1.4, 5.6).

d To solve $f(x) = 0$, look to see where the curve crosses the x-axis or $f(x) = 0$.

Solutions are −2.4, 0 and 2.4.

Solving an equation using an exponential graph

C A

a Draw the graph of $3x + 4y = 12$ for values of x from -2 to 4.

b On the same axes, draw the graph of $y = 2^x$ for values of x from -2 to 2.

c Write down the coordinates of the point of intersection of the line and the curve.

Solution

a Make a table of values for $3x + 4y = 12$, using $x = -2$, 0 and 4.

[Hint: Plot the end values, plus $x = 0$ because it is easy to substitute.]

x	-2	0	4
y	4.5	3	0

Plot the points and join them with a straight line.

b Make a table of values for $y = 2^x$ for all integer values of x from -2 to 2.

x	-2	-1	0	1	2
y	0.25	0.5	1	2	4

Plot the points on the same grid.
Join them with a smooth curve.

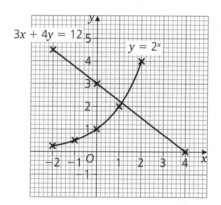

c The point of intersection is (1.1, 2.2).

Practise 8.1 – 8.3

1 10 Swiss francs (CHF) = 8.2 euros (EUR)

    a Use this information to draw a graph to convert Swiss francs to euros.

            [Grade E]

    b Use your conversion graph to convert 4.5 Swiss francs to euros.

            [Grade E]

    c Explain how you could use the graph to convert 27 Swiss francs to euros.

            [Grade D]

2 This speed–time graph shows a three hour truck journey.

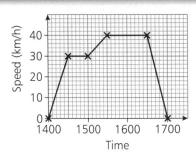

a Find the acceleration of the truck between 1400 and 1430.

[Grade B]

b What is happening between 1530 and 1630?

[Grade C]

c Find the deceleration of the truck between 1630 and 1700.

[Grade B]

d Find the total distance travelled.

[Grade B]

3 a Find the equation of the line *PQ*.   [Grade C]

b *PQR* is a straight line and *Q* is the midpoint of *PR*.

Work out the coordinates of *R*.

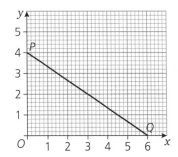

[Grade C]

4 a Copy and complete the table of values for $y = 2x^2 + x - 6$.   [Grade C]

x	−3	−2	−1	0	1	2	3
2x²	18		2			8	18
y	9		−5			4	15

b Draw the graph of $y = 2x^2 + x - 6$ for values of *x* from −3 to 3.

[Grades E–C]

c Use your graph to solve the equation $2x^2 + x - 6 = 0$.

[Grade C]

d By drawing a suitable line, estimate the gradient of the graph at the point where $x = 1$.

[Grade B]

5 $f(x) = \dfrac{2}{x}$ and $g(x) = \dfrac{2x + 1}{2}$

a Draw the graph of $y = f(x)$ for values of *x* from −3 to 3 ($x \neq 0$).

[Grades E–C]

b On the same grid, draw the graph of $y = g(x)$.

[Grade D]

c Use your graphs to write down two solutions of the equation $f(x) = g(x)$.

[Grade C]

Transformations

Revise 9.1 Symmetry

2-D symmetry

Line symmetry

A 2-D shape has line symmetry when it can be folded so that one half fits *exactly* over the other. The **line of symmetry** is like a mirror line where each side of the shape is reflected at the other side.

Rotational symmetry

A shape has **rotational symmetry** if it *looks exactly the same* when it is rotated by less than 360° to a *new* position. The **order of rotational symmetry** is the number of different positions in which it looks the same during a complete turn.

Special 2-D shapes and their symmetries

The symmetries of some special shapes are shown below:

Equilateral triangle	Isosceles triangle	Scalene triangle
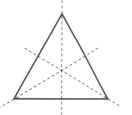	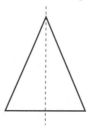	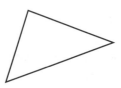
3 lines of symmetry	1 line of symmetry	No lines of symmetry
Rotational symmetry of order 3	No rotational symmetry	No rotational symmetry
	(order 1)	(order 1)

Square

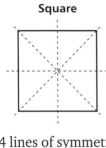

4 lines of symmetry
Rotational symmetry
of order 4

Rectangle

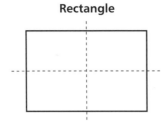

2 lines of symmetry
Rotational symmetry
of order 2

Rhombus

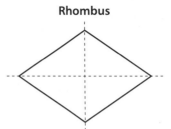

2 lines of symmetry
Rotational symmetry
of order 2

Parallelogram

No lines of symmetry
Rotational symmetry of
order 2

Trapezium

No lines of symmetry
No rotational symmetry
(order 1)

Isosceles trapezium

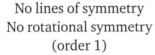

This shape has
2 parallel sides
and 2 equal sides.

1 line of symmetry
No rotational symmetry
(order 1)

Kite

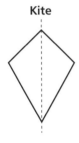

1 line of symmetry
No rotational symmetry
(order 1)

Circle

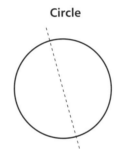

Every diameter of a circle
is a line of symmetry.
It looks the same when
rotated through any angle.

A circle has an infinite number of lines of symmetry.
The order of its rotational symmetry is also infinite.

Regular pentagon

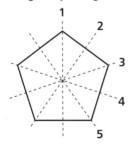

5 lines of symmetry
Rotational symmetry
of order 5

Regular hexagon

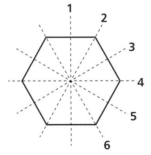

6 lines of symmetry
Rotational symmetry
of order 6

Regular octagon

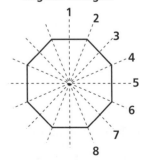

8 lines of symmetry
Rotational symmetry
of order 8

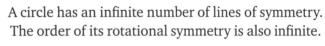

In general, a regular n-sided polygon has n lines of symmetry and rotational symmetry of order n.

3-D Symmetry

Plane symmetry

A plane is a flat surface. A **plane of symmetry** divides a 3-D shape into two equal halves. Each half is the reflection of the other half in the plane of symmetry.

The diagrams below show the three planes of symmetry of a cuboid.

Plane of symmetry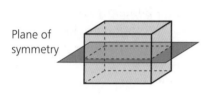

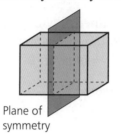

Plane of symmetry

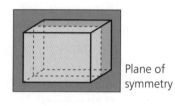

Plane of symmetry

Rotational symmetry

The cuboid also has rotational symmetry of order 2 about each of the axes shown.

This means that the cuboid will look exactly the same in *two different positions* as it rotates through a complete turn about the axis.

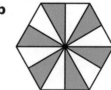

Axis

Axis

Axis

 Worked examples

Recognising 2-D symmetry

a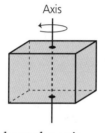

b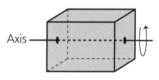

For each diagram, write down: **i** the order of rotational symmetry

ii the number of lines of symmetry.

Solution

a **i** This diagram looks the same if you rotate it by 180°.

It has rotational symmetry of order 2.

ii The diagram has 2 lines of symmetry.

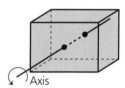

1 --- Line of symmetry

2

The 2 halves match if you fold along either of these lines.

b **i** This diagram has rotational symmetry of order 6.

　　ii It is not possible to fold this diagram so that the two halves match.

　　　The diagram has no lines of symmetry.

> **Exam tip**
>
> Remember that you can use tracing paper to find or check the answers in transformation or symmetry questions.

Using 2-D symmetry
E

a A triangle has one line of symmetry.

　　i What is the geometrical name of this triangle?

　　ii One angle of the triangle is 100°. Find the other angles.

b A quadrilateral has two parallel sides and one line of symmetry.

　　i What is the geometrical name of this quadrilateral?

　　ii One angle of the quadrilateral is 100°. Find the other angles.

Solution

a **i** A triangle with one line of symmetry is an isosceles triangle.

　　ii The angle sum of a triangle is 180°, so there can only be one angle of 100°.

　　　The sum of the other 2 angles must be 80°.

　　　Each angle = 80° ÷ 2 = 40°

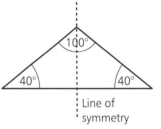

b **i** The quadrilateral is an isosceles trapezium.

　　ii The line of symmetry means there must be another angle of 100°.

　　　The sum of interior angles on parallel lines is 180°, so the other two angles are both 80°.

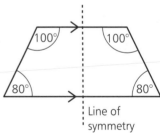

> You can check the angles by adding them – the angles of the quadrilateral should add up to 360°.

Recognising 3-D symmetry
C

Write down:

a the order of rotational symmetry of this cone about the axis shown

b the number of planes of symmetry of the cone.

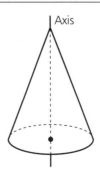

Solution

a The cone will look the same if it rotates through any angle about the axis shown.

The order of rotational symmetry of the cone about this axis is infinite.

b The cone also has an infinite number of planes of symmetry (like that shown in the diagram).

Each plane of symmetry cuts the cone exactly in half.

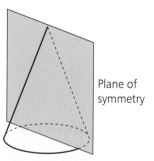

Plane of symmetry

Revise 9.2 Reflections, rotations and translations

Reflection

In a **reflection**, each point on the **object** is **mapped** onto a point on the **image** that is on the other side of the **mirror line**. The object and image points are an equal distance from the mirror line.

On this grid, flag F is mapped onto flag A by a reflection in the x-axis. Reflection in $x = 4$ maps F onto B.

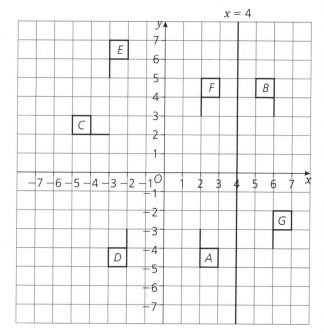

Rotation

In a **rotation**, the object is rotated clockwise or anticlockwise around a **centre of rotation**.

Flag F is mapped onto flag C by a rotation of $90°$ anticlockwise (or $270°$ clockwise) about the origin, $(0, 0)$. A rotation of $180°$ clockwise or anticlockwise about the origin maps F onto D.

Translation

In a **translation**, the object moves across the page without being rotated or reflected. The translation is sometimes described by a **vector**.

A translation by vector $\begin{pmatrix} -5 \\ 2 \end{pmatrix}$, maps F onto E. A translation by vector $\begin{pmatrix} 4 \\ -7 \end{pmatrix}$, maps F onto G.

The top number in the vector gives the horizontal movement with positive being right and negative left. The bottom number gives the vertical movement with positive being up and negative down.

Worked examples

Reflections

A triangle has vertices at $A(-5, 4)$, $B(-1, 6)$ and $C(-6, 8)$.

a Draw the reflection of triangle ABC in the line $y = 4$. Label the image $A_1 B_1 C_1$.

b Draw the reflection of triangle ABC in the line $x = -2$. Label the image $A_2 B_2 C_2$.

c Draw the reflection of triangle ABC in the line $y = x$. Label the image $A_3 B_3 C_3$.

Solution

Triangle ABC is shown on the grid.

a The mirror line, $y = 4$, goes through points such as $(-1, 4)$, $(0, 4)$, $(1, 4)$ and $(2, 4)$.

Reflecting each vertex of triangle ABC in this mirror line gives the image $A_1 B_1 C_1$.

b The mirror line, $x = -2$, goes through points such as $(-2, -1)$, $(-2, 0)$, $(-2, 1)$ and $(-2, 2)$.

Reflecting each vertex of triangle ABC in this mirror line gives the image $A_2 B_2 C_2$.

c The mirror line, $y = x$ is the line through points such as $(-8, -8)$, $(-4, -4)$, $(0, 0)$, $(4, 4)$ and $(8, 8)$.

Reflecting each vertex of triangle ABC in this mirror line gives the image $A_3 B_3 C_3$.

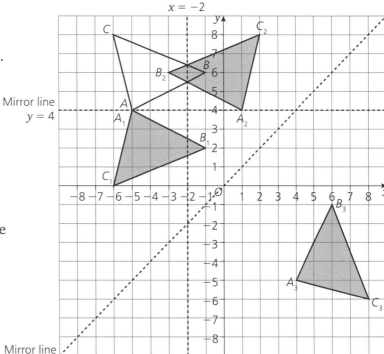

$x = -2$ is parallel to the y-axis.
$y = 4$ is parallel to the x-axis.
$y = x$ is a diagonal line as shown.

Exam tip

Remember that if a is a constant then:

- a line with equation $x = a$ is parallel to the y-axis.

- a line with equation $y = a$ is parallel to the x-axis.

The y-axis is also the line $x = 0$.

The x-axis is also the line $y = 0$.

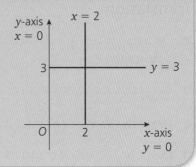

Rotations

Kite K has vertices at $(0, -1)$, $(2, 1)$, $(4, -1)$ and $(2, -5)$.

a Draw the image of kite K after a rotation of 90° clockwise about the point $(2, -5)$.

Label the image A.

b Draw the image of kite K after a rotation of 180° clockwise about the point $(3, 0)$.

Label the image B.

c Draw the image of kite K after a rotation of 270° anticlockwise about the point $(2, 4)$.

Label the image C.

Solution

The kite K and its images are shown on the grid.

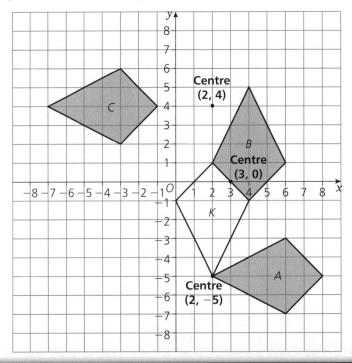

Exam tip

Remember that you can use tracing paper to find or check your answers.

Translations

a On axes for $0 \leqslant x \leqslant 10$ and $0 \leqslant y \leqslant 8$, join points $(2, 3)$, $(3, 3)$, $(4, 4)$, $(3, 5)$ and $(1, 4)$ to give a pentagon P.

b Draw the image of P after a translation by vector $\binom{6}{3}$. Label the image P_1.

c Draw the image of P_1 after a translation by vector $\binom{-2}{-5}$. Label the image P_2.

d Describe the single translation which maps the image P_2 onto the original pentagon P.

Solution

a The axes and pentagon P are as shown.

b The translation by vector $\begin{pmatrix} 6 \\ 3 \end{pmatrix}$ moves the pentagon, P, 6 units to the right and 3 units upwards.

This gives the image P_1.

c The translation by vector $\begin{pmatrix} -2 \\ -5 \end{pmatrix}$ moves P_1 by 2 units to the left and 5 units downwards to P_2.

d The movement from P_2 to P is 4 units to the left and 2 units upwards.

So P_2 is mapped onto the original pentagon P by a translation by vector $\begin{pmatrix} -4 \\ 2 \end{pmatrix}$.

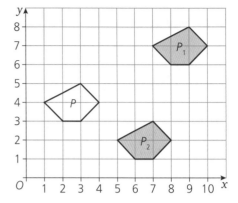

Revise 9.3 Enlargements, stretches and shears

Enlargement

In an **enlargement**, the **object** is enlarged by a **scale factor**.

- When the scale factor is greater than 1, the image is bigger than the object.
- When the scale factor is between 0 and 1, the image is smaller than the object.
- When the scale factor equals 1, the image is the same size as the object.

The lines joining each point and its image all meet at the **centre of enlargement**.

To find the image of a point, multiply the distance from the centre to the point by the scale factor.

- When the scale factor is negative, measure from the centre in the opposite direction to find the image.

Triangle T is mapped onto A by an enlargement with centre $(-7, 1)$ and scale factor 2.

T is mapped onto B by an enlargement with centre the origin (O), and scale factor -2.

T is mapped onto C by an enlargement with centre $(-3, -3)$ and scale factor $\frac{1}{2}$.

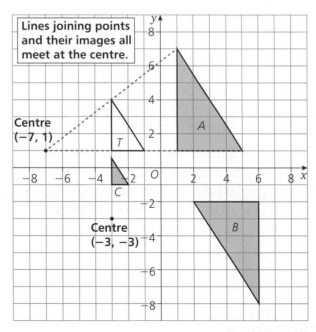

Stretches

One-way stretch

In a one-way **stretch**, points on an **invariant line** do not move. All other points move in a direction *perpendicular* to the invariant line. The distance moved by a point is proportional to its distance from the invariant line.

In the diagram pentagon *P* is mapped onto *A* by a one-way stretch with scale factor 2 and the *y*-axis invariant.

Two-way stretch

In a two-way stretch, there are two invariant lines and the shape is stretched in two directions.

The diagram shows a square *S* and its image *B* after a two-way stretch. *S* is stretched horizontally with invariant line $x = -6$ and scale factor 4 and also stretched vertically with the *x*-axis invariant and scale factor $\frac{1}{2}$.

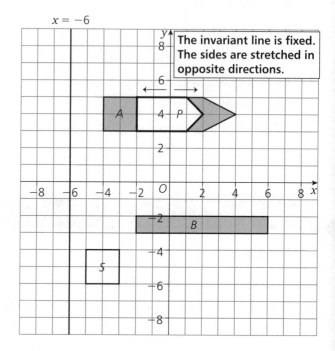

The invariant line is fixed. The sides are stretched in opposite directions.

Shears

In a **shear** points on an invariant line are fixed. All other points move in a direction *parallel* to the invariant line. The distance moved by a point is proportional to its distance from the invariant line.

The diagram shows triangle *T* and its image *A* after a shear with the *y*-axis invariant.
Point (1, 1) moves down by one unit to (1, 0).
Point (3, 1) is three times as far from the *y*-axis, so it moves down by 3 units to (3, −2).

When the invariant line divides an object into two parts, the parts move in opposite directions. Rectangle *R* is mapped onto *B* by a shear which moves (1, −4) to (4, −4) with invariant line $y = -5$.

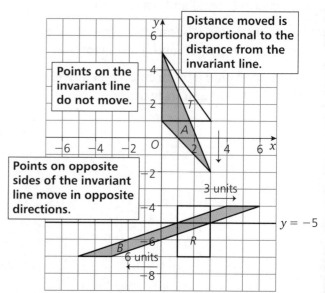

Distance moved is proportional to the distance from the invariant line.

Points on the invariant line do not move.

Points on opposite sides of the invariant line move in opposite directions.

Describing and combining transformations

To describe a **transformation** *fully*, give all the details listed in the table.

To describe a:	You must give:
reflection, M	the position of the mirror line
rotation, R	the angle of rotation the direction (clockwise or anticlockwise) the centre of rotation
translation, T	the vector (or the distance and direction)
enlargement, E	the scale factor the centre of enlargement
stretch, S	the type (one-way or two-way) the invariant line(s) the scale factor(s)
shear, H	the invariant line the image of one point that is not on the invariant line

Exam tip

For full marks in the exam you must give a full description.

The transformations listed in the table above can be represented by the letters shown. These letters can then be combined to represent a combination of transformations. The order of the letters is very important. For example, the image of a point or shape, P, after a translation T is represented by $T(P)$. If that image is then reflected by M, the final image is represented by $MT(P)$. So MT represents translation T, *followed by* reflection M.

Worked examples

Enlargements and stretches

C A

A parallelogram has vertices at $P(1, 2)$, $Q(3, 2)$, $R(4, 3)$ and $S(2, 3)$.

a **i** Draw the image of $PQRS$ after enlargement with scale factor 3 and centre P.

Label the image $P_1Q_1R_1S_1$.

ii Find the ratio of the area of $PQRS$ to the area of $P_1Q_1R_1S_1$, giving your answer in its simplest form.

b **i** Draw the image of $PQRS$ after a one-way stretch with the x-axis invariant and P mapped onto the point $P_2(1, 6)$. Label the image $P_2Q_2R_2S_2$.

ii Find the ratio of the area of $PQRS$ to the area of $P_2Q_2R_2S_2$, giving your answer in its simplest form.

Solution

a i The centre of the enlargement, P, does not move in the enlargement.

The distance from P to each of the other vertices is multiplied by 3.

Joining these image points gives the parallelogram $P_1Q_1R_1S_1$.

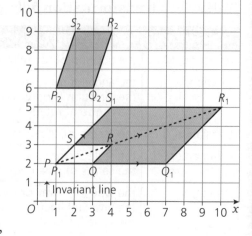

ii The ratio of lengths in $PQRS$ to lengths in $P_1Q_1R_1S_1$ is $1:3$.

$P_1Q_1R_1S_1$ is similar to $PQRS$, so the ratio of the area of $PQRS$ to the area of $P_1Q_1R_1S_1$ is $1:3^2 = 1:9$.

b i In the one-way stretch, the invariant line is the x-axis, so this does not move.

$P(1, 2)$ is 2 units above the x-axis and moves to $P_2(1, 6)$. This is 3 times as far from the x-axis.

The scale factor of the stretch is 3.

$Q(3, 2)$ is also 2 units above the x-axis, so it moves to $Q_2(3, 6)$.

$R(4, 3)$ and $S(2, 3)$ are both 3 units above the x-axis.

Their images are 9 units above the x-axis at $R_2(4, 9)$ and $S_2(2, 9)$.

ii The parallelogram is stretched by scale factor 3 in only one direction.

The base of the parallelogram is not changed, but the height is multiplied by 3.

This means the area of the image is 3 times as big.

The ratio of the area of $PQRS$ to the area of $P_2Q_2R_2S_2$ is $1:3$.

Exam tip

Always try to use the quickest method. If you have time, use an alternative method to check your answer.

You can check the ratios by finding the area of each parallelogram:

Area of $PQRS$ = base × height = 2 × 1 = 2 square units.

Area of $P_1Q_1R_1S_1$ = 6 × 3 = 18 square units.

Area of $P_2Q_2R_2S_2$ = 2 × 3 = 6 square units.

The ratio of the area of $PQRS$ to the area of $P_1Q_1R_1S_1$ = $2:18 = 1:9$.

The ratio of the area of $PQRS$ to the area of $P_2Q_2R_2S_2$ = $2:6 = 1:3$.

Shears

A

$A(3, 1)$, $B(5, 1)$, $C(5, 3)$ and $D(4, 3)$ are the vertices of trapezium $ABCD$.

a In a shear the x-axis is invariant and $(1, 1)$ maps to $(-3, 1)$.

Draw the image of $ABCD$ after this shear. Label the image $A_1B_1C_1D_1$.

b A shear has invariant line $x = 2$ and maps $(1, 1)$ to $(1, 3)$.

Draw the image of $ABCD$ after this shear. Label the image $A_2B_2C_2D_2$.

Solution

In a shear the distance moved by each point is proportional to its distance from the invariant line.

The tables below give the images of the vertices after each shear and the diagram shows the results.

a

Point	Distance from x-axis	Distance moved	Image
(1, 1)	1 unit above	4 units ←	(−3, 1)
A(3, 1)	1 unit above	4 units ←	A_1(−1, 1)
B(5, 1)	1 unit above	4 units ←	B_1(1, 1)
C(5, 3)	3 units above	12 units ←	C_1(−7, 3)
D(4, 3)	3 units above	12 units ←	D_1(−8, 3)

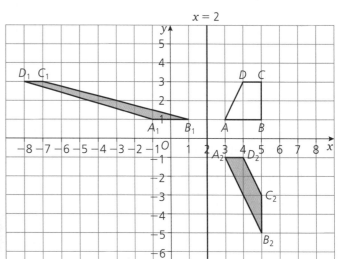

b

Point	Distance from $x = 2$	Distance moved	Image
(1, 1)	1 unit left	2 units ↑	(1, 3)
A(3, 1)	1 unit right	2 units ↓	A_2(3, −1)
B(5, 1)	3 units right	6 units ↓	B_2(5, −5)
C(5, 3)	3 units right	6 units ↓	C_2(5, −3)
D(4, 3)	2 units right	4 units ↓	D_2(4, −1)

Combining transformations

B

Triangle T has vertices at (−4, 1), (−4, 3) and (−3, 3).

R is rotation through 90° clockwise about the origin. M is reflection in the line $y = x$.

a Using axes with $-5 \leqslant x \leqslant 5$ and $-1 \leqslant y \leqslant 5$, draw the image MR($T$).

b Describe fully a single transformation which maps T onto MR(T).

Solution

a

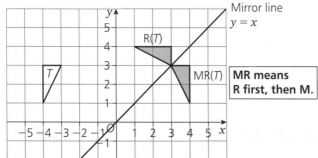

Rotating T through 90° clockwise about the origin gives R(T).

Reflecting R(T) in the line $y = x$ then gives MR(T).

b The single transformation which maps T onto MR(T) is reflection in the y-axis (or $x = 0$ line).

Describing transformations

a Describe fully the transformation that maps the letter F to:

   i shaded image *A*

   ii shaded image *B*

   iii shaded image *C*

   iv shaded image *D*.

b Describe fully the transformation that maps the letter L to:

   i shaded image *P*

   ii shaded image *Q*

   iii shaded image *R*

   iv shaded image *S*.

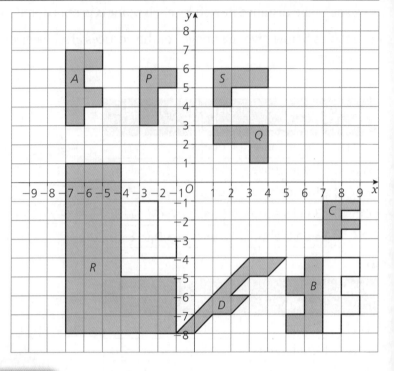

> ### Exam tip
>
> For *full marks* you must give a *full* description.

Solution

a **i** The letter F moves 14 units to the left and 11 units upwards to give shaded image *A*.

    The transformation is a translation by vector $\begin{pmatrix} -14 \\ 11 \end{pmatrix}$.

  ii The letter F is rotated through a half turn to give shaded image *B*.

    The point $(7, -6)$ stays in place, so this is the centre of the rotation.

    The transformation is a rotation of 180° clockwise (or anticlockwise) about the point $(7, -6)$.

  iii The shaded image *C* is the same width as F, but half as tall.

    So the transformation is a vertical one-way stretch with scale factor $\frac{1}{2}$.

    The invariant line must be horizontal and twice as far from F as from *C*.

    The transformation is one-way, with invariant line $y = 2$ and scale factor $\frac{1}{2}$.

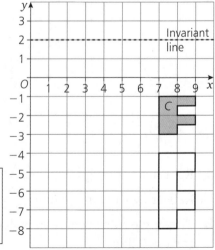

> The line $y = 2$ is twice as far from points on F than from their image points on C.

iv

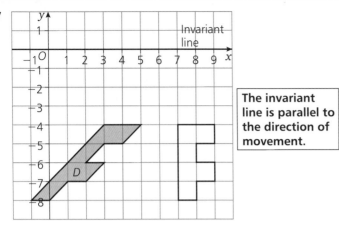

> The invariant line is parallel to the direction of movement.

The transformation that maps the F onto D is a shear.

Points on the top of the F move horizontally by 4 units.

Points 1 unit below this move by 5 units.

The invariant line is a horizontal line 4 units above the top of the F.

The transformation is a shear with the x-axis invariant and which maps $(7, -4)$ to $(3, -4)$.

b i The letter L is reflected in the line $y = 1$ to give shaded image P.

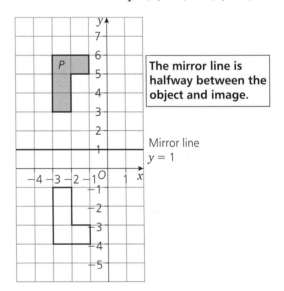

> The mirror line is halfway between the object and image.

Mirror line $y = 1$

ii The letter L is reflected in the line $y = -x$ to give shaded image Q.

> You can check by tracing and folding along the mirror line.

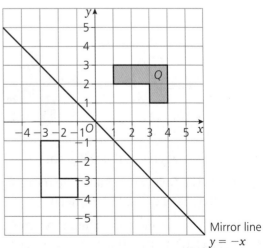

Mirror line $y = -x$

iii The sides of shaded image *R* are three times as long as the letter L.

The transformation is an enlargement with centre $(-1, -2)$ and scale factor 3.

> To find the centre, draw lines joining each vertex and its image.

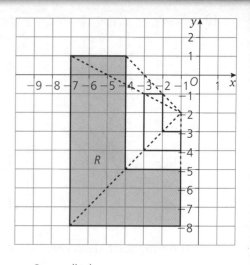

iv The transformation that maps the letter L onto shaded letter *S* is a rotation of 90° clockwise (or 270° anticlockwise) about the point $(4, -1)$.

> Use tracing paper or perpendicular bisectors to find the centre.

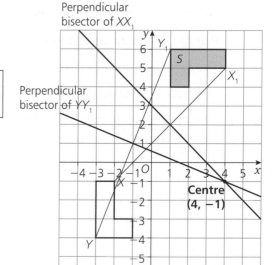

Exam tip

To find a difficult centre of rotation, draw the perpendicular bisectors of lines joining points and their images. The perpendicular bisectors meet at the centre of rotation.

Practise 9.1 – 9.3

1 For each diagram below, write down:

   i the number of lines of symmetry   **ii** the order of rotational symmetry.

a    **b**    **c**   **d**

[Grades E–D]

2 Make two copies of this diagram.

  a On the first copy, shade one more square so that there is one line of symmetry.

  b On the second copy, shade two more squares so that there is rotational symmetry of order 2.

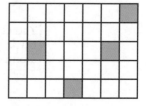

[Grade D]

3 a Quadrilateral *A* has rotational symmetry of order 2, but no lines of symmetry.

    i Sketch quadrilateral *A* and write down its geometrical name.

    ii Mark on your sketch the equal sides and angles of the shape.

    iii One angle of quadrilateral *A* is 50°. Find the other angles.

b Quadrilateral *B* has 1 line of symmetry, but no rotational symmetry.

  The diagonals of quadrilateral *B* are not equal in length.

    i Sketch quadrilateral *B* and write down its geometrical name.

    ii Mark on your sketch the equal sides and angles of the shape.

    iii Quadrilateral *B* has two angles of 105°.

  One of the remaining angles is twice the size of the other. Find these angles.   [Grades E–D]

4 a On axes of *x* and *y* from −8 to 8, draw the quadrilateral with vertices at (2, 4), (4, 4), (4, 5) and (1, 6). Label the quadrilateral *A*.

b Draw the image of *A* after reflection in the line $y = -1$. Label this image *B*.

c Draw the image of *A* after reflection in the line $x = -2$. Label this image *C*.

d Draw the image of *A* after rotation through 90° clockwise about the origin. Label this image *D*.

e Draw the image of *A* after rotation through 180° clockwise about the point (4, 4). Label this image *E*.

f Draw the image of *A* after translation by vector $\binom{4}{2}$. Label the image *F*.

g Draw the image of *A* after translation by vector $\binom{-8}{-7}$. Label the image *G*.

h Draw the image of *A* after enlargement with centre (4, 7) and scale factor 3. Label this image *H*.   [Grades D–C]

5 Describe fully the single transformation which maps:

a *A* onto *B*

b *A* onto *C*

c *A* onto *D*

d *B* onto *E*

e *B* onto *H*

f *F* onto *G*

g *H* onto *I*

h *D* onto *G*

i *I* onto *J*

j *E* onto *K*.

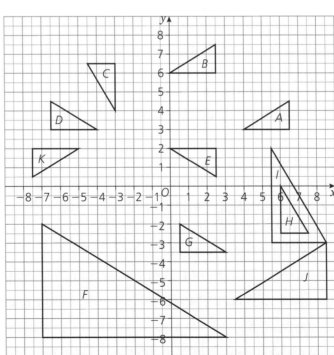

[Grades D–C]

6 For each 3-D shape write down:

   i the number of planes of symmetry

   ii the order of rotational symmetry about the axis shown.

   a Hexagonal prism   **b** Square-based pyramid   **c** Cylinder

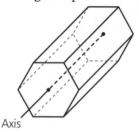
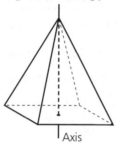
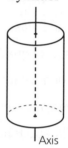

Axis   Axis   Axis   [Grade C]

7 a On axes of x and y from -7 to 7, draw the kite with vertices at $A(2, 1)$, $B(1, 0)$, $C(2, -3)$ and $D(3, 0)$.

   i Draw the image of $ABCD$ after enlargement with scale factor 2 and centre A. Label the image $A_1B_1C_1D_1$.

   ii Find the ratio, area of $ABCD$: area of $A_1B_1C_1D_1$ in its simplest form.

   b **i** Draw the image of $ABCD$ after a one-way stretch with $x = 7$ invariant and scale factor 2. Label the image $A_2B_2C_2D_2$.

   ii Draw the image of $ABCD$ after a one-way stretch with $y = 7$ invariant and scale factor $\frac{1}{2}$. Label the image $A_3B_3C_3D_3$.

   iii Find the ratio, area of $ABCD$: area of $A_2B_2C_2D_2$: area of $A_3B_3C_3D_3$ in its simplest form.

[Grades C–A]

8 a On axes of x and y from -6 to 6 draw:

   i the square $ABCD$ with vertices $A(-2, 2)$, $B(0, 4)$, $C(-2, 6)$ and $D(-4, 4)$

   ii the square $PQRS$ with vertices $P(4, -4)$, $Q(6, -2)$, $R(4, 0)$ and $S(2, -2)$.

   b Describe fully the single transformation which maps:

   i $ABCD$ onto $PQRS$ (remember the order of the letters is important: A must map onto P, B onto Q, C onto R and D onto S)

   ii $ABCD$ onto $QRSP$ **iii** $ABCD$ onto $RSPQ$ **iv** $ABCD$ onto $SPQR$ **v** $ABCD$ onto $SRQP$.

[Grade C]

9 a On axes of x and y from -8 to 8 draw the triangle ABC, the square $KLMN$ and the pentagon $PQRST$. The coordinates of the vertices of these shape are given below:

$A(2, 0)$, $B(2, 3)$, $C(4, 3)$, $K(5, -4)$, $L(7, -4)$, $M(7, -6)$, $N(5, -6)$, $P(-7, 1)$, $Q(-4, 1)$, $R(-2, 2)$, $S(-4, 3)$, $T(-7, 3)$.

   b A shear with x-axis invariant maps $(0, 1)$ onto $(1, 1)$.

   i Draw the image of triangle ABC in this shear. Label the image $A_1B_1C_1$.

   ii Draw the image of square $KLMN$ in this shear. Label the image $K_1L_1M_1N_1$.

   c A shear with invariant line $x = -4$ maps P onto $P_1(-7, -8)$.

   Draw the image of pentagon $PQRST$ in this shear. Label the image $P_1Q_1R_1S_1T_1$.   [Grade A]

10 a Describe fully the single
   transformation which maps
   rectangle R onto

   i A **ii** B.

   b Describe fully the single
   transformation which maps
   trapezium T onto

   i C **ii** D.

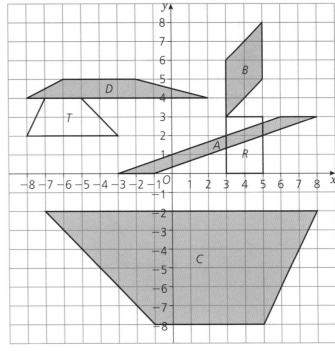

[Grades B–A]

11 Trapezium T has vertices at $(5, 2)$, $(8, 2)$, $(7, 4)$ and $(5, 4)$.

   M is reflection in the line $x = 3$. N is reflection in the line $y = -x$.

   a Using axes with $-8 \leqslant x \leqslant 8$ and $-5 \leqslant y \leqslant 5$, draw the image NM($T$).

   b Describe fully a single transformation which maps T onto NM(T).

[Grade B]

12 For this question use axes of x and y from -8 to 8.

   Q is the quadrilateral with vertices at $(2, 2)$, $(3, 2)$, $(5, 5)$ and $(2, 4)$.

   R_1 is rotation clockwise through $90°$ about the origin.

   R_2 is rotation clockwise through $90°$ about the point $(2, -1)$.

   M is reflection in the x-axis. T is translation by the vector $\begin{pmatrix} -9 \\ 5 \end{pmatrix}$.

   a Describe fully a single transformation which maps Q onto R_1M(Q).

   b Describe fully a single transformation which maps Q onto TR_2(Q).

[Grade B]

10 More number

Learning outcomes

After this chapter you should be able to:

- round numbers to 10, 100, … or to a specified number of decimal places or significant figures | F | E | D |
- round answers to a reasonable accuracy in the context of a given problem | D |
- make estimates of numbers, quantities and lengths | E | D |
- give appropriate upper and lower bounds for data to a specified degree of accuracy and use these in calculations | C | B | A |
- calculate squares, square roots, cubes and cube roots of numbers | F | E |
- use and interpret positive, negative and zero and fractional indices and use the rules of indices | D | C | B | A |
- use and convert to and from standard form | C | B |
- recognise patterns in sequences and relationships between different sequences | E | D | C |
- find a term-to-term rule in a sequence | E |
- write the terms of a sequence or a series of diagrams given the nth term | D | C |
- write the nth term of a linear sequence or series of diagrams | C | B |
- use language, notation and Venn diagrams to describe sets and represent relationships between sets | C | B | A |
- define a set in a variety of ways | C | B |
- understand and use set notation. | C | B | A | A* |

Revise 10.1 Estimation and accuracy

Rounding

Whole numbers

Numbers can be **rounded** to the nearest **integer** (whole number) or to the nearest power of 10, e.g. 10, 100 or 1000.

To round to the nearest 10, for example, look at the number in the next place value (units) column.

Round *up* if this number is 5 or more.

Round *down* if this number is less than 5.

Similarly, to round to the nearest 100, look in the tens column, and to round to the nearest 1000, look in the hundreds column.

Numbers can also be rounded to a given number of decimal places or **significant figures**.

Decimal places

Decimal places are counted from the right of the decimal point.

To round to 2 decimal places, for example, look at the 3rd decimal place.

If this digit is 5 or more, round *up*.

If this digit is less than 5, round *down*.

Significant figures

Significant figures are counted from the first non-zero digit, ignoring the position of the decimal point.

Ignore any zeros at the front of the number as they are not significant.

For example,

Rounding 236.5396 to the nearest hundredth gives

$$236.53|96 = 236.54 \text{ (to the nearest hundredth)} \longleftarrow \boxed{\text{Round up}}$$

Rounding 236.5396 to 4 significant figures gives

$$236.5|396 = 236.5 \text{ (to 4 s.f.)}$$

Rounding 236.5396 to 3 decimal places gives

$$236.539|6 = 236.540 \text{ (to 3 d.p.)} \longleftarrow \boxed{\text{Round up}}$$

You must show 3 decimal places so fill in the third place with a zero.

Estimating

When using a calculator to find the answers, it is useful to estimate your answer first.

This is usually done by rounding each number to one significant figure.

This estimate should be close to your calculated answer. It often shows you quickly if you have made a mistake by entering numbers incorrectly or pressing the wrong calculator key.

Upper and lower bounds

The **upper** and **lower bounds** are the maximum and the minimum values of the number before rounding.

When a number has been rounded, you can work backwards to find the numbers it could have been before rounding.

For example, a number has been rounded to the nearest centimetre. You can find the upper and lower bounds by taking half of this (0.5 cm) and adding it to and subtracting it from the number.

When you are given a number that has been rounded, and have not been told to what it has been rounded, then always give your answer to the next degree of accuracy.

For example, 34.24 has been given to 2 decimal places or 4 significant figures. The upper and lower bounds should be given to 3 decimal places or 5 significant figures.

Watch out for ambiguous questions where the rounded value gives you no indication as to how it has been rounded, e.g. 27 000 could have been rounded to the nearest 1000, to the nearest 100, to the nearest 10 or to the nearest unit.

> **Exam tip**
>
> In the examination, you are often asked to give the answers as inequalities.
>
> For example:
>
> minimum length $\leqslant$ length $<$ maximum length
>
> $14.75\,\text{cm} \leqslant$ length $< 14.85\,\text{cm}$
>
> Notice the two different inequalities used. The maximum length itself cannot be reached but you still refer to this as the upper bound.

Upper and lower bounds in calculations

You must be able to use upper and lower bounds in calculations involving addition, subtraction, multiplication and division. You will then be asked to find the overall maximum and minimum values.

When adding:

overall maximum = upper bound of A + upper bound of B

overall minimum = lower bound of A + lower bound of B

When subtracting:

overall maximum = upper bound of A − lower bound of B

overall minimum = lower bound of A − upper bound of B

When multiplying:

overall maximum = upper bound of A × upper bound of B

overall minimum = lower bound of A × lower bound of B

When dividing:

$$\text{overall maximum} = \frac{\text{upper bound of A}}{\text{lower bound of B}}$$

$$\text{overall minimum} = \frac{\text{lower bound of A}}{\text{upper bound of B}}$$

When substituting into formulae or calculations involving more than one operation, you will need to think carefully about how to combine the upper and lower bounds.

Worked examples

Estimating

D

$$\frac{472 \times 0.247}{0.98 + 1.492}$$

a Estimate the value of this calculation.

b Use your calculator to find the value of the original calculation correct to three significant figures.

Solution

a $\dfrac{4|72 \times 0.2|47}{0.9|8 + 1|.492}$

Round each number correct to one significant figure.

This gives:

$$\dfrac{500 \times 0.2}{1 + 1}$$

$$= \dfrac{100}{2}$$

$$= 50$$

b $\dfrac{472 \times 0.247}{0.98 + 1.492}$

$$= 47.1\,|\,618123...$$

$$= 47.2 \text{ (to 3 s.f.)}$$

Upper and lower bounds

c

The Sydney Harbour Bridge is 1149 metres in length (to the nearest metre).

a Copy and complete the following statement:

    ___ m ⩽ length < ___ m

b This bridge is said to be the tallest bridge of its kind in the world. It measures 134 metres from the top of the bridge to the level of the water.

If this height had been measured to the nearest 0.5 metre, copy and complete the following statement:

    ___ cm ⩽ height < ___ cm

Solution

a The length of the bridge has been rounded to the nearest metre.

So the upper and lower bounds are half of this, 0.5 m, to each side of 1149 m.

The upper bound is 1149 + 0.5 = 1149.5 m.

The lower bound is 1149 − 0.5 = 1148.5 m.

So

    1148.5 m ⩽ length < 1.149.5 m

b The height of the bridge has been rounded to the nearest 0.5 m.

The answer is required in centimetres so 134 m = 13 400 cm

100 cm = 1 m

So the upper and lower bounds are half of this, 0.25 m or 25 cm, to each side of 13 400 cm.

The upper bound is 13 400 + 25 = 13 425 cm.

The lower bound is 13 400 − 25 = 13 375 cm.

So

    13 375 cm ⩽ height < 13 425 cm

Calculating with upper and lower bounds

A moving walkway at the airport is 358 metres long, correct to 3 significant figures.

It moves at a speed of 2.4 metres per second, correct to 1 decimal place.

a Write down the upper and lower bounds for:

   i the length of the walkway   **ii** the speed of the walkway.

b Use your answers from part **a** to complete the inequality for the maximum and minimum possible times taken for a piece of luggage to travel from one end of the walkway to the other.

        _____ seconds $\leqslant$ time $<$ _____ seconds

Give your answers to the nearest second.

Solution

a **i** The length has been rounded to 3 significant figures, so

      upper bound $= 358.5$ metres   lower bound $= 357.5$ metres

   ii The speed of the walkway has been rounded to 1 decimal place, so

      upper bound $= 2.45$ metres per second   lower bound $= 2.35$ metres per second

b Time (in seconds) $= \dfrac{\text{length (in metres)}}{\text{speed (in metres per second)}}$

     Maximum time $= \dfrac{\text{maximum length}}{\text{minimum speed}}$

              $= \dfrac{358.5}{2.35}$ seconds

              $= 152.55319...$ seconds

              $= 153$ seconds or 2 minutes and 33 seconds (to the nearest second)

     Minimum time $= \dfrac{\text{minimum length}}{\text{maximum speed}}$

              $= \dfrac{357.5}{2.45}$ seconds

              $= 145.91836...$ seconds

              $= 146$ seconds or 2 minutes and 26 seconds (to the nearest second)

    146 seconds $\leqslant$ time $<$ 153 seconds

Revise 10.2 Indices and standard form

Squares and cubes

Squares and square roots

A **square number** is the number you get when you multiply a number by itself, e.g. $7 \times 7 = 49$.

It can be written in **index notation** as 7^2.

The opposite or **inverse** of squaring is finding the **square root**.

$7^2 = 49$ so $\sqrt{49} = 7$ or -7

However the $\sqrt{}$ sign usually means find the positive square root.

Cubes and cube roots

A **cube number** is the number you get when you multiply three of the same number together,

e.g. $4 \times 4 \times 4 = 64$.

It can be written in index notation as 4^3.

The opposite or inverse of cubing is finding the **cube root**.

$4^3 = 4 \times 4 \times 4 = 64$ $\Rightarrow \sqrt[3]{64} = 4$

Indices and powers

Index form can also be used to show higher powers than 2 or 3:

$6^5 = 6 \times 6 \times 6 \times 6 \times 6$

The **index** or **power** tells you how many times the **base number** has to be multiplied by itself.

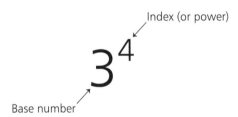

Index (or power)

Base number

You say this as '3 to the power of 4'.

So 3^4 means $3 \times 3 \times 3 \times 3 = 81$.

When finding a root of a number other than 2 or 3 on a calculator, use one of the following keys:

The rules of indices

1. When *multiplying* powers of the same number, *add* the indices:

    $a^m \times a^n = a^{m+n}$

2. When *dividing* powers of the same number, *subtract* the indices:

    $a^m \div a^n = a^{m-n}$

3. To *raise a power* of a number to another power, *multiply* the indices:

    $(a^m)^n = a^{m \times n}$

Negative indices

Negative indices can be written as the corresponding positive index of the reciprocal:

$$a^{-n} = \frac{1}{a^n}$$

Zero indices

Zero indices always have a value of 1:

$$a^0 = 1$$

Fractional indices

Fractional indices involve finding roots of numbers:

$$a^{\frac{1}{n}} = \sqrt[n]{a}$$

and $\quad a^{\frac{m}{n}} = \sqrt[n]{a^m} \text{ or } (\sqrt[n]{a})^m$

Standard form

A number is in **standard form** if it is written in the form:

A power of 10 where n is an integer.

$$A \times 10^n$$

A can be equal to 1 but cannot be equal to 10.

Standard form is used to write down very large and very small numbers. This makes them easier to use when doing calculations.

> **Exam tip**
>
> Large numbers, when rewritten in standard form, will always be multiplied by a positive power of 10.
> Small numbers, when rewritten in standard form, will always be multiplied by a negative power of 10.

Converting to standard form

You should make sure that you can convert an ordinary number into standard form and a number in standard form back to an ordinary number.

Adding, subtracting, multiplying and dividing numbers in standard form

When calculating with numbers in standard form, you may need to use the rules of indices mentioned earlier.

> **Exam tip**
>
> When calculating with numbers in standard form, it is useful to put brackets around the number. This makes it easier to see what you are doing, e.g. $(5 \times 10^3) \times (3 \times 10^4)$.

Worked examples

Indices

Simplify

a $6p^3 \times 2p^{-2}$ **b** $15q^2 \div 5q^{-3}$ **c** $(2r^{-3})^2$ **d** $\left(\dfrac{27}{125}x^{21}\right)^{\frac{1}{3}}$ **e** $\dfrac{(16p^8)^{\frac{1}{2}} \times 2p^{-1}}{64p^{\frac{2}{3}}}$

Solution

Always deal with the whole numbers separately from the indices.

a $6p^3 \times 2p^{-2} = 12p^{3 + (-2)} = 12p^{3-2} = 12p$ ◄─── | Using the 1st rule of indices. |

b $15q^2 \div 5q^{-3} = \dfrac{15}{5}q^{2 - (-3)} = 3q^{2+3} = 3q^5$ ◄─── | Using the 2nd rule of indices. |

c $(2r^{-3})^2 = (2^2)(r^{-3})^2 = 4r^{-3 \times 2} = 4r^{-6}$ or $\dfrac{4}{r^6}$ ◄─── | Using the 3rd rule of indices. |

d $\left(\dfrac{27}{125}x^{21}\right)^{\frac{1}{3}} = \dfrac{3}{5}x^7$

e $\dfrac{(16p^8)^{\frac{1}{2}} \times 2p^{-1}}{64p^{\frac{2}{3}}} = \dfrac{4p^4 \times 2p^{-1}}{64p^{\frac{2}{3}}} = \dfrac{8p^3}{64p^{\frac{2}{3}}} = \dfrac{1}{8}p^{3 - \frac{2}{3}} = \dfrac{1}{8}p^{\frac{7}{3}}$

Standard form

a Write the following two numbers in standard form:

    789 000 000 and 0.000543

b Calculate the following, giving your answers in standard form:

   i $(7.2 \times 10^4) \times (5 \times 10^{-3})$

   ii $(6.5 \times 10^4) + (3.2 \times 10^3)$

Solution

a 789 000 000 ◄─── | 7.89 is between 1 and 10. |

    $= 7.89 \times 10^8$ ◄─── | To get from 789 000 000 to 7.89, the number has moved 8 places right. |

    0.000543 ◄─── | 5.43 is between 1 and 10. |

    $= 5.43 \times 10^{-4}$ ◄─── | To get from 0.000543 to 5.43, the number has moved 4 places left. |

b You may use a calculator to find these answers, but the solutions below show how they can be found without a calculator.

   i $(7.2 \times 10^4) \times (5 \times 10^{-3})$

       $= 7.2 \times 5 \times 10^4 \times 10^{-3}$ ◄─── | Multiply the first part of each number together. |

       $= 36 \times 10^{4 + (-3)}$ ◄─── | Use the 1st rule of indices. |

       $= 36 \times 10^1$

       $= 3.6 \times 10^1 \times 10^1$ ◄─── | Write 36 as 3.6×10^1. |

       $= 3.6 \times 10^2$ ◄─── | Use the 1st rule of indices again. |

ii $(6.5 \times 10^4) + (3.2 \times 10^3)$

$\qquad = 65\,000 + 3200$

$\qquad = 68\,200$

$\qquad = 6.82 \times 10^4$ ◄──────────────── | Write 68 200 in standard form. |

Using standard form in calculations

| B |

A particular pine tree pollen consists of minute spherical grains each 55 micrometres (μm) in diameter.

a Write down the diameter of a grain in metres.

b Find the volume of 200 of these grains in micrometres cubed (μm^3).

c Convert the answer to part **b** into a volume in m^3.

Give all your answers in standard form correct to one decimal place.

Solution

a 1 micrometre $= \dfrac{1}{1\,000\,000}$ metre $= 1 \times 10^{-6}$ metre

$\quad$ 55 micrometres $= 55 \times 10^{-6} = 5.5 \times 10^{-5}$ metre

b Volume of a sphere $= \frac{4}{3}\pi r^3$ ◄──────────── | Radius $= 0.5\,\mu m$ |

$\qquad\qquad\qquad = \frac{4}{3} \times \pi \times 0.5^3\,\mu m^3$

$\qquad\qquad\qquad = 0.5235...\,\mu m^3$

$\quad$ Volume of 200 spheres $= 200 \times 0.5235...\,\mu m^3$

$\qquad\qquad\qquad\qquad = 104.7197...\,\mu m^3$

$\qquad\qquad\qquad\qquad = 1.0 \times 10^2\,\mu m^3$ (to 1 d.p.)

c $\quad 1\,m = 10^6\,\mu m$

$\quad 1\,\mu m = 1 \times 10^{-6}\,m$

$\quad 1\,\mu m^2 = (10^{-6})^2\,m^2$

$\quad 1\,\mu m^3 = (10^{-6})^3\,m^3$

$\quad$ So volume of 200 spheres $= 1.0 \times 10^2 \times 10^{-18}\,m^3$

$\qquad\qquad\qquad\qquad\qquad = 1.0 \times 10^{-16}\,m^3$ (to 1 d.p.)

Revise 10.3 Numbers and sequences

The rules of a sequence

A **sequence** is a set of numbers or patterns with a given **rule** or pattern, e.g. 1, 4, 9, 16, 25.

Each number in the sequence is called a **term**.

The sequences can be shown using patterns or diagrams.

If a sequence goes on for ever, it is called an **infinite** sequence.

This is shown by a series of dots, e.g. 3, 6, 9, 12, … .

A rule can be written in two different ways: as a **term-to-term rule** or using a formula for the **nth term**.

The term-to-term rule

A term-to-term rule explains how you get from one term to the next in the sequence.

The rule could be 'divide by 2' or 'subtract 5'.

It could also be a combination of two parts, such as 'divide by 4 and then add on 3'. Be careful as order matters.

Each term is compared to the next term.

If you were asked for the 100th term, you would need to know the 98th, 97th, and so on.

This would take a long time.

The formula for the nth term

It is easier to compare the term with its position in the sequence.

This is sometimes called the **position-to-term rule**.

This will give a formula for the nth term.

First, find the common difference between **consecutive** terms.

This is used to find the formula.

You will find it easier to construct a table, but there are other methods you can use.

All sequences solved in this way are called **linear sequences**.

Once you have found the formula for the nth term, you can find any term easily, including the 100th term, by substitution.

Linear sequences have common constant differences of the form $+d$ or $-d$.

If a = first term and d = difference, then

$$n\text{th term} = \text{difference} \times n + (\text{first term} - \text{difference})$$
$$= dn + (a - d)$$

Other common sequences

You should also be able to recognise the following sequences:

1, 4, 9, 16, 25, ...	Squares
1, 8, 27, 64, 125, 216, ...	Cubes
1, 2, 4, 8, 16, ...	The next term is double the previous term
$1, \frac{1}{2}, \frac{1}{3}, \frac{1}{4}, ...$	Reciprocals
1, 3, 6, 10, 15, ...	Triangular numbers
1, 1, 2, 3, 5, 8, ...	Fibonacci sequences, where each term is the sum of the previous two terms

Worked examples

Finding the nth term

C

a Find the nth term of the sequence:

$$3, \quad 7, \quad 11, \quad 15, \quad 19, \quad ...$$

b Find the value of the hundredth term.

c Using your previous answers, find the value of the hundredth term of this sequence:

$$2, \quad 6, \quad 10, \quad 14, \quad 18, \quad ...$$

Solution

a The nth term is found by comparing the term to its position in the sequence: 1st, 2nd, 3rd, etc.

```
     1st   2nd   3rd   4th   5th
      3     7    11    15    19
        +4    +4    +4    +4
```

When finding this nth term, it is still useful to know the difference between the terms of the sequence.

The above diagram shows that the common difference between the terms is 4. This means that there is a $4n$ in the nth term.

n	1st	2nd	3rd	4th
Sequence	3	7	11	15
$4n$	4 −1	8 −1	12 −1	16 −1

To return to the original sequence from the $4n$ row, you need to subtract 1 from each number.

The nth term of the sequence is $4n - 1$.

b To find the value of the 100th term, replace n by 100 in the formula for the nth term:

$$\text{value of 100th term} = 4 \times 100 - 1$$
$$= 400 - 1$$
$$= 399$$

c Every number in the new sequence is one less than the corresponding number in the previous sequence.

So instead of the nth term being $4n - 1$, the nth term is $4n - 2$.

This also means that:

$$\text{value of 100th term} = 4 \times 100 - 2$$
$$= 400 - 2$$
$$= 398$$

Comparing sequences

The nth term of the sequence:

$$3, \quad 4, \quad 7, \quad 12, \quad 19, \quad \ldots$$

is $(n - 1)^2 + 3$.

Write down the formula for the nth term of the sequence:

$$6, \quad 9, \quad 14, \quad 21, \quad 30, \quad \ldots$$

Simplify your answer.

Solution

$$3, \quad 4, \quad 7, \quad 12, \quad 19, \quad \ldots$$
$$6, \quad 9, \quad 14, \quad 21, \quad 30, \quad \ldots$$

Comparing the sequences

$$
\begin{array}{ccccc}
3 & 4 & 7 & 12 & 19 \\
+3\downarrow & +5\downarrow & +7\downarrow & +9\downarrow & +11\downarrow \\
6 & 9 & 14 & 21 & 30
\end{array}
$$

The differences are $3, 5, 7, 9, 11, \ldots$.

Each of these numbers in the sequence of differences increases by 2, so there is a $2n$ in the formula.

The nth term of the sequence of differences is $2n + 1$.

The nth term for the sequence $6, 9, 14, 21, 30, \ldots$ is $(n - 1)^2 + 3 + 2n + 1$

This simplifies to $n^2 - 2n + 1 + 3 + 2n + 1 = n^2 + 5$.

Check

When $n = 1$, 1st term is $1^2 + 5 = 6$.

When $n = 2$, 2nd term is $2^2 + 5 = 9$, and so on.

Patterns in sequences

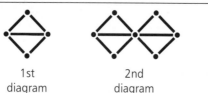

| | 1st diagram | 2nd diagram | 3rd diagram |

a Copy and complete the table showing the total number of lines and the number of dots enclosed in each pattern:

Diagram	1st	2nd	3rd	4th	5th
Lines	5	10	15		
Dots	4	7			

b Find the nth term for: **i** the number of lines used   **ii** the number of dots used.

c From your previous answers, show that the nth term for the total number of lines and dots is $8n + 1$.

d Which diagram has a total number of 137 dots and lines?

Solution

a

Diagram	1st	2nd	3rd	4th	5th
Lines	5	10	15	**20**	**25**
Dots	4	7	**10**	**13**	**16**

b   **i**   The numbers in the second row, labelled lines, are exactly 5 times the diagram numbers.

So the nth term of the sequence for the number of lines is $5n$.

You could also obtain this answer by noticing that the common difference between the terms of the sequence is always 5.

ii   Comparing each term with the next, the common difference is 3.

This means that there is a $3n$ in the nth term.

Diagram	1st	2nd	3rd	4th	5th
Dots	4	7	10	13	16
$3n$	3 +1	6 +1	9 +1	12 +1	15 +1

To return to the original sequence from the $3n$ row, you need to add 1 to each number.

The nth term of the sequence for the number of dots is $3n + 1$.

c nth term for lines $= 5n$

nth term for dots $= 3n + 1$

So adding these expressions gives:

nth term for total number of lines and dots $= 8n + 1$

Diagram	1st	2nd	3rd	4th	5th
Lines	5	10	15	20	25
Dots	4	7	10	13	16
Lines + dots	9	17	25	33	41

d The number of lines and dots in the nth diagram $= 8n + 1$. This is equal to 137.

So $\quad 8n + 1 = 137$

$\qquad\quad 8n = 137 - 1 \quad \longleftarrow$ | Subtract 1 from each side. |

$\qquad\quad 8n = 136$

$\qquad\quad n = \dfrac{136}{8}$

$\qquad\quad n = 17$

The 17th diagram has a total of 137 lines and dots.

Revise 10.4 Set notation

Set notation

A **set** is a collection of objects or numbers, usually having something in common.

The members of a set are called the **elements** of the set.

Set notation

A set is named with a capital letter, for example, set **A**.

The **membership** of the set is all the elements in the set.

The symbol $\in$ means 'is an element of'

$\qquad\qquad \notin$ means 'is not an element of'.

A set can contain items or numbers.

It can also contain **ordered pairs**. These are pairs that go together, like coordinates.

The members of a set can be listed or defined, for example,

A $= \{1, 2, 3, 4, 6, 12\}$ $\quad$ is the same as $\quad$ **A** $= \{x : x$ is a factor of $12\}$

Venn diagrams

A **Venn diagram** is a way of showing the elements of sets in a diagram.

A rectangle represents the **Universal Set**, written as $\mathscr{E}$.

This is the set containing all the elements to be considered.

Other sets are shown as circles.

Combining sets

$\mathscr{E} =$ Universal Set

C is contained in **A**.

So **C** is a **subset** of **A**, or **C** $\subseteq$ **A**.

If **A** contains **C** and has elements not in **C**, then **C** is a **proper subset** of **A**, or **C** $\subset$ **A**.

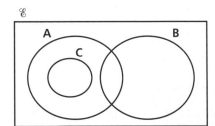

The **union** of A and B, **A ∪ B**, is everything in **A** or **B** (all of the shaded sections put together).

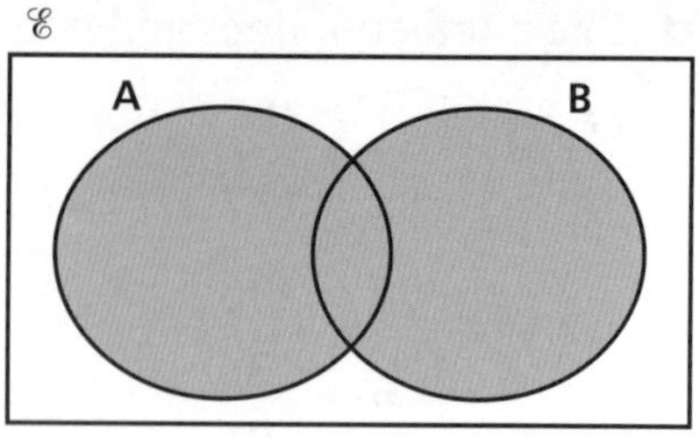

The **intersection** of A and B, **A ∩ B**, is everything in *both* **A** and **B** (the shaded section).

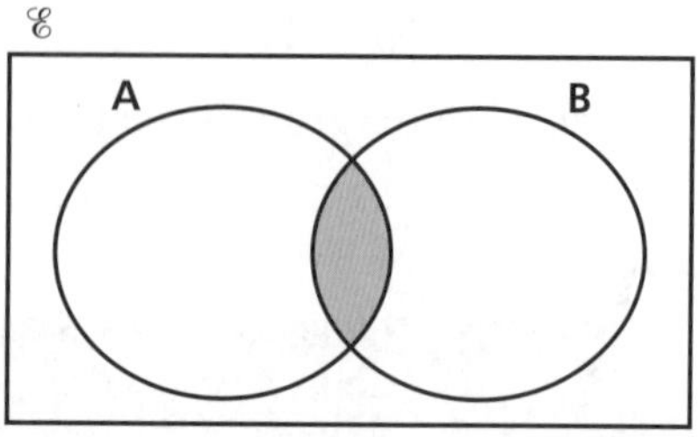

An **empty set**, or **null set**, ∅, is one that contains no elements.

The **complement** of set A, A′, is the set of everything not in set **A** (the shaded section).

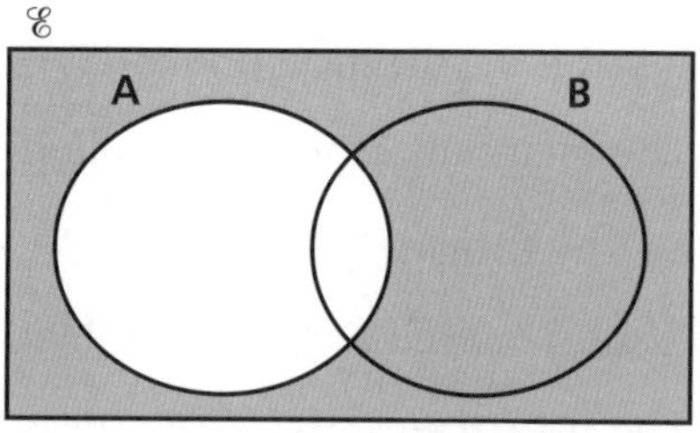

Worked examples

Drawing and interpreting Venn diagrams

B

$\mathscr{E} = \{x : x \in \mathbb{N}, x < 11\}$

A = {x: x is an even number}

B = {x: x is a factor of 10}

C = {x: x is a factor of 12}.

a List the elements of: **i** A **ii** A′ **iii** A ∩ B.

b Show this information in a Venn diagram.

c List the elements of (A ∪ C)′.

Solution

$\mathscr{E} = \{1, 2, 3, 4, 5, 6, 7, 8, 9, 10\}$

A = {2, 4, 6, 8, 10}

B = {1, 2, 5, 10}

C = {1, 2, 3, 4, 6}

Exam tip

List the elements of each set before drawing the Venn diagram.

a **i** A = {2, 4, 6, 8, 10} **ii** A′ = {1, 3, 5, 7, 9} **iii** A ∩ B = {2, 10}

b

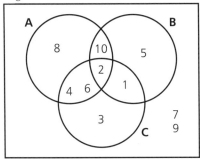

$(A \cup C) = \{1, 2, 3, 4, 6, 8, 10\}$

c So $(A \cup C)' = \{5, 7, 9\}$

Venn diagrams can also be used to show the number of elements in a set.

Number of elements in a set

A

There are 35 people working in an office.

18 wear glasses (**G**), 20 wear a watch (**W**) and 9 wear neither glasses nor a watch.

Show this information on a Venn diagram.

Solution

9 people wear neither glasses nor a watch.

These go outside the glasses and watch circles on the Venn diagram.

So there are $35 - 9 = 26$ in $G \cup W$.

There are 20 in **W**, so there must be $26 - 20 = 6$ in $G \cap W'$.

So there are $18 - 6 = 12$ in $G \cap W$.

That leaves 8 in $W \cap G'$.

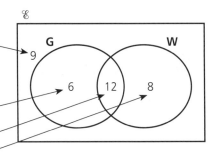

Practise 10.1 – 10.4

1 $(0.321 + 0.192)^2 \times 438 - \sqrt{3.92}$

  a Write all the numbers in the above calculation correct to one significant figure.

  b Use your answers to estimate the value of the calculation.

  c Use your calculator to find the value of the original calculation, correct to 4 significant figures.

[Grade D]

2 a Write down the first five terms of each of these sequences:

    i 1st term = 7, rule = +6

    ii 1st term = 9, rule = −4

    iii 1st term = 1, rule = ×2, then +1.

  b The nth term of a sequence is $\dfrac{n}{n^2 + 1}$.

    Write down the first five terms of the sequence.

[Grade D]

3 The population of Shanghai in the 2000 census was assessed at being 16 737 734.

  a Rewrite this population correct to:

    i the nearest 10 000

    ii the nearest 100.

  b In 2010, the population had increased to 23 020 000 (to the nearest ten thousand).

    Copy and complete the following statement:

    _____ ⩽ population < _____

  c The actual population in 2010 was stated as 23 019 148.

    Find the percentage increase in population from 2000 to 2010.

    Give your answer correct to 1 decimal place.

[Grade C]

4 The population of Nepal in July 2011 was 2.97×10^7.

The area of Nepal is $1.47 \times 10^5 \text{ km}^2$.

Work out the average number of people per km^2 in July 2011.

Give your answer as an ordinary number.

[Grade C]

5 a Write the following ordinary numbers in standard form:

    i 17 400   **ii** 0.005328.

  b Write the following numbers, given in standard form, as ordinary numbers:

    i 3.254×10^6 **ii** 3.254×10^{-5}.

[Grade C]

6 a **i** Write down the next two terms in the sequence: 15, 9, 3, −3, ….

    ii State the rule for finding the next two terms in the sequence.

    iii Find the expression for the nth term in the sequence.

  b Write down an expression for the nth term of this sequence: 3, 9, 15, 21, 27, ….

  c Add together the expressions for both sequences.

[Grade C]

7

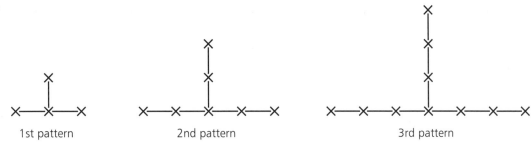

1st pattern   2nd pattern   3rd pattern

a Copy and complete the table below:

Pattern	1st	2nd	3rd	4th	5th
Lines	3	6			
Crosses	4	7			

b In pattern 7, write down the number of:

    i lines   **ii** crosses.

c For the nth pattern, write down the nth term for:

    i the number of lines   **ii** the number of crosses.

d How many crosses are in the 50th pattern?

e How many lines are there in the pattern with 76 crosses?

[Grade C]

8 Write each of these four numbers on the Venn diagram:

    3.4 $\sqrt{36}$ $\sqrt{35}$ $\dfrac{5}{\sqrt{9}}$

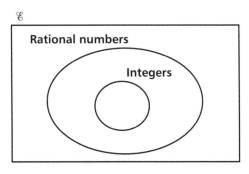

[Grade C]

9 The formula for the nth term of the sequence:

    $1\frac{3}{5}$,   3, $4\frac{4}{5}$,   7,   ...

is $\dfrac{(n+1)(n+3)}{k}$, where k is an integer.

a Find the value of k.

b Test your formula when $n = 3$. Show your working.

c Find the value of the 74th term in the sequence.

[Grade B]

10 To raise money for charity, Fariah walks 28 km (correct to the nearest km). She does this every day for 7 days.

   a Copy and complete the statement below:

     _____ $\leqslant$ distance walked in 1 day $<$ _____

   b Fariah was sponsored for a total of $2.5 per kilometre walked.

     Find the maximum and the minimum amount of money that Fariah had raised at the end of 7 days. Give your answer correct to the nearest dollar.

                                         [Grade B]

11 $n(\mathscr{E}) = 35$, $n(A) = 18$, $n(A \cap B) = 7$ and $n(A' \cap B) = 6$.

Complete the Venn diagram to show this information.

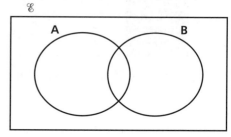

                                         [Grade B]

12 $\mathscr{E} = \{x : x \in \mathbb{N}, x \leqslant 12\}$

   $A = \{x : x \text{ is a prime number}\}$

   $B = \{x : x \text{ is a square number}\}$

   $C = \{x : x \text{ is a multiple of 3}\}$

   Draw a Venn diagram to show this information.

                                         [Grade B]

13 **a** The diameter of a red blood cell is 7 μm.

     1 μm is called a micrometre and is equal to $\dfrac{1}{1\,000\,000}$ metre.

     Write down the diameter of the red blood cell in metres and in standard form.

   b Use the formula:

$$A = \frac{B^{\frac{3}{2}}}{C^2}$$

     to calculate A, when $B = 1.44 \times 10^6$ and $C = 4.8 \times 10^5$.

     Give your answer in standard form.

                                         [Grade A]

14 On the Venn diagrams, shade the regions:

   a $A' \cap B$ **b** $A' \cup B$.

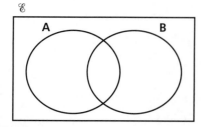 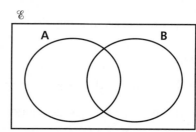

                                         [Grade B]

15 a Find the value of p when $3^p \times 3^2 = 3^7$.

   b Find the value of q when $\dfrac{8^q}{8^4} = 8^{11}$.

   c Find the value of r when $4^r = \dfrac{1}{64}$.

   d Find the value of s when $512^{-\frac{2}{3}} = 2^s$.

   e Find the value of t when $125 = (25)^{2t-1}$.

[Grades B–A*]

16 A solid metal cylinder is of height 15 cm (to the nearest cm) and diameter 8.7 cm (to the nearest mm).

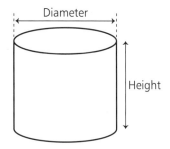

   a Copy and complete the following statements:

     i _____ $\leqslant$ height $<$ _____   Give your answers correct to 1 d.p.

     ii _____ $\leqslant$ radius $<$ _____   Give your answers correct to 3 d.p.

   b The density of the metal is 7.8 g/cm³, correct to one decimal place.

     Find the maximum and the minimum mass of the cylinder, correct to the nearest g/cm³ (take $\pi = 3.14$).

   c Now use 3.142 for π.

     Find the percentage increase in the maximum mass of the cylinder. Give your answer correct to the nearest hundredth of a percent.

[Grade A*]

11 Probability

Revise 11.1 Probability

Equally likely outcomes

Something that is **impossible** has a probability of 0.

Something that is **certain** has a probability of 1.

All other probabilities lie between 0 and 1.

When two or more events have the same probability, they are called **equally likely outcomes**.

A coin is just as likely to land on heads as on tails.

A dice is just as likely to land on a 1, or a 2, or a 3, or a 4, or a 5, or a 6.

These are equally likely outcomes.

When outcomes are all equally likely,

$$\text{probability of an event} = \frac{\text{number of outcomes for the event}}{\text{total number of possible outcomes}}$$

A short way of writing 'The probability of a spinner landing on 4' is P(4).

$P(4) = \frac{1}{6}$ ← The number of successful outcomes is 1 and the total number of possible outcomes is 6.

Exam tip

You can write probabilities as fractions, decimals or percentages. Do not write probabilities as ratios.

To find the probability of an outcome *not* happening, use the formula:

probability of an outcome not happening = 1 − probability of the outcome happening

So, P(not 4) = $1 - \frac{1}{6} = \frac{5}{6}$

Experimental probability

When outcomes are not equally likely, a probability can be found by experiment.

You can use experimental data by repeating an experiment a large number of times.

These experiments are called **trials**.

The **relative frequency** is defined by the formula:

$$\text{relative frequency} = \frac{\text{number of outcomes for the event}}{\text{total number of trials}}$$

If an experiment is repeated a large number of times, the relative frequency becomes the **experimental probability**.

To find the experimental probabilities of some events, you have to rely on historical data. You do this by looking at the frequencies of similar events in the past, such as particular weather conditions or patterns in the behaviour of a volcano.

Combined events

Sample space diagrams

A **sample space diagram** is a list or table of all possible outcomes.

Sample space diagrams are very useful when studying two events.

The addition rule

When more than one outcome is a successful outcome, the individual probabilities are added.

For example, the probability of a dice landing on an even number is $\frac{3}{6}$, and the probability of it landing on a 5 is $\frac{1}{6}$.

The probability of it landing on *either* an even number *or* a 5 is:

$$\text{P(even)} + \text{P(5)} = \tfrac{3}{6} + \tfrac{1}{6} = \tfrac{4}{6} = \tfrac{2}{3}$$

> **Exam tip**
>
> The addition rule is the OR rule, when one thing OR another is required.

This is only true for **mutually exclusive** events.

Mutually exclusive events have no common outcomes.

For example, rolling an even number or a multiple of 3 are *not* mutually exclusive events.

This is because 6 is an even number *and* is a multiple of 3, so it can belong with either event.

The multiplication rule

To find the probability of two events both happening, the individual probabilities are multiplied.

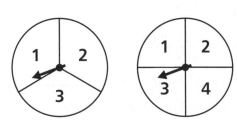

The two-way table shows you that the probability of both spinners landing on 2 is $\frac{1}{12}$.

		Four-part spinner			
		1	2	3	4
Three-part spinner	1				
	2				
	3				

P(both 2) = P(three-part spinner is 2) × P(four-part spinner is 2)

$$= \frac{1}{3} \times \frac{1}{4} = \frac{1}{12}$$

Tree diagrams

When all the outcomes are not equally likely, a **tree diagram** can be used.

A tree diagram shows all the outcomes for each event, and the probabilities.

Separate sets of branches are used for each event.

The probabilities are written on each branch.

Worked examples

Equally likely outcomes

E

A bag contains tiles that spell the word:

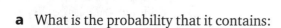

| T | E | L | E | P | H | O | N | E |

A tile is chosen at random.

a What is the probability that it contains:

　i the letter E

　ii a letter from the first half of the alphabet?

b What is:

　i P(not E)

　ii P(a letter from the second half of the alphabet)?

Solution

a　**i**　There are 9 tiles, and 3 show the letter E.

So, $p(E) = \dfrac{\text{number of ways of chosing a letter E}}{\text{total number of tiles}} = \frac{3}{9} = \frac{1}{3}$

　ii　The letters from the first half of the alphabet are E, L, E, H, E.

So P(a letter from the first half of the alphabet) $= \frac{5}{9}$

b **i** $P(\text{not } E) = 1 - P(E) = 1 - \frac{1}{3} = \frac{2}{3}$

ii $P(\text{a letter from the second half of the alphabet})$

$= 1 - P(\text{a letter from the first half of the alphabet})$

$= 1 - \frac{5}{9} = \frac{4}{9}$

Experimental probability

C

A company makes batteries.

They test a sample to see how long they last.

The results are shown in the table below:

Battery life, h (hours)	$0 < h \le 20$	$20 < h \le 40$	$40 < h \le 60$	$60 < h \le 80$	$80 < h \le 100$	$100 < h \le 120$
Frequency	7	27	51	129	75	11

a What is the experimental probability of a battery lasting between 80 and 100 hours?

b What is the experimental probability of a battery lasting more than 60 hours?

c The company makes 35 000 batteries in a week. How many would you expect to last more than 80 hours?

Solution

a They tested $7 + 27 + 51 + 129 + 75 + 11 = 300$ batteries.

75 lasted between 80 hours and 100 hours,

so the experimental probability is $\frac{75}{300} = \frac{1}{4}$ ← Cancelling by 75 makes the fraction simpler and easier to understand.

b $129 + 75 + 11 = 215$ lasted more than 60 hours.

The experimental probability is $\frac{215}{300} = \frac{43}{60}$ ← Cancelling by 5

c 86 lasted more than 80 hours, so you might expect $\frac{86}{300}$ of 35 000 to last more than 80 hours, or 10 033 to the nearest whole number.

Using a sample space diagram

C B

Marcus is playing a game with two dice.

One is numbered 1, 2, 3, 4, 5 and 5.

The other is numbered 1, 2, 3, 4, 4, 4.

a Draw a sample space diagram to show this information.

b Use the sample space diagram to find:

i the probability that the sum of the two dice is even

ii the most likely sum, and the probability of that sum.

Solution

a

		First dice					
		1	**2**	**3**	**4**	**5**	**5**
Second dice	**1**	2	3	4	5	6	6
	2	3	4	5	6	7	7
	3	4	5	6	7	8	8
	4	5	6	7	8	9	9
	4	5	6	7	8	9	9
	4	5	6	7	8	9	9

b i 16 out of 36 outcomes are even, so P(even) $= \frac{16}{36} = \frac{4}{9}$.

ii The most common score is 6, with a probability of $\frac{7}{36}$.

Tree diagram

C A

A bag contains 5 blue discs and 3 red discs.

Nadira chooses a disc at random. She notes the colour and then replaces it.

Khalid then chooses a disc at random.

a i Show this information on a probability tree.

ii Calculate the probability that both discs chosen are the same colour.

b If instead of replacing it, Nadira keeps her disc. Now calculate the probability that both discs are the same colour.

Solution

a i

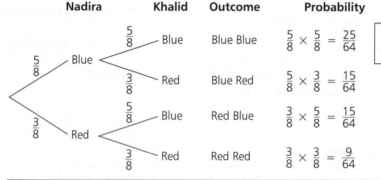

| Nadira | Khalid | Outcome | Probability |

Multiply the probabilities as both events must happen.

On each set of branches, the probabilities will always add up to 1.

ii P(both the same colour) = P(both blue) + P(both red)

$$= \frac{25}{64} + \frac{9}{64}$$

$$= \frac{34}{64} = \frac{17}{32}$$

Cancel by 2 to give the answer in its simplest form.

Add the probabilities because one OR the other outcome is required.

b Khalid's probabilities depend on the colour of Nadira's disc:

If Nadira chooses a blue disc, there are 4 blue discs and 3 red discs for Khalid to choose from. But if Nadira chooses a red disc, Khalid chooses from 5 blue discs and 2 red discs.

Nadira	Khalid	Outcome	Probability
	$\frac{4}{7}$ Blue	Blue Blue	$\frac{5}{8} \times \frac{4}{7} = \frac{20}{56} = \frac{5}{14}$
$\frac{5}{8}$ Blue	$\frac{3}{7}$ Red	Blue Red	$\frac{5}{8} \times \frac{3}{7} = \frac{15}{56}$
$\frac{3}{8}$ Red	$\frac{5}{7}$ Blue	Red Blue	$\frac{3}{8} \times \frac{5}{7} = \frac{15}{56}$
	$\frac{2}{7}$ Red	Red Red	$\frac{3}{8} \times \frac{2}{7} = \frac{6}{56} = \frac{3}{28}$

P(both the same colour) = P(both blue) + P(both red)

$$= \frac{5}{14} + \frac{3}{28}$$

$$= \frac{10}{28} + \frac{3}{28} = \frac{13}{28}$$

Practise 11.1

1 A bag of fruit contains 6 apples, 3 bananas, 1 pear and 2 oranges.

Augusta takes one piece of fruit at random.

What is the probability that she gets:

a a banana

b a mango?

[Grade E]

2 A bag contains some discs.

12 discs are red, 8 discs are blue and 5 discs are yellow.

A disc is chosen at random.

Find, as a fraction, the probability of each of the following events:

a The disc is red.

b The disc is red or yellow.

c The disc is not yellow.

[Grades E–D]

3 A bag contains some red counters, some blue counters and some green counters.

The probability of choosing a red counter at random is $\frac{2}{11}$.

The probability of choosing a blue counter at random is $\frac{5}{11}$.

a Find the probability of choosing a green counter.

b There are 8 red counters in the bag.

How many counters are there altogether?

[Grades D–C]

4 A ball is rolled down a slope with nails.

The ball eventually falls into one of five boxes, labelled A, B, C, D or E.

Sadiq rolls the ball 50 times.

The table shows his results:

Box	A	B	C	D	E
Frequency	6	10	15	13	6

Mouna rolls the ball 200 times. Here are her results:

Box	A	B	C	D	E
Frequency	15	51	72	49	13

a Use Sadiq's results to calculate the probability that the ball falls:

i into box A

ii into box C

iii not into box C.

b Use Mouna's results to calculate the probability that the ball falls:

i into box A

ii into box C

iii not into box C.

c Whose results do you think give more accurate probabilities? Give a reason for your answer.

[Grade C]

5 A factory tests a sample of switches.

The switches are switched on and off repeatedly until they break.

The results are shown below.

Number of times switched, n	Number that broke
$0 \leqslant n < 500$	11
$500 \leqslant n < 1000$	4
$1000 \leqslant n < 1500$	5
$1500 \leqslant n < 2000$	7
$2000 \leqslant n < 2500$	9
$2500 \leqslant n < 3000$	11
$3000 \leqslant n < 3500$	14
$3500 \leqslant n < 4000$	17
$n \geqslant 4000$	22

a Calculate the probability that a switch will break between 3000 and 3500 uses.

b If the company make 6000 switches in a week, how many are likely to break in under 1000 uses?

[Grade C]

6 There are 15 counters, all the same size, in a bag.

Seven are blue, five are white and the rest are red.

Melissa takes a counter without looking, records its colour and replaces it in the bag. She then does this a second time.

Find the probability that:

a the first counter taken is red

b the first counter taken is red or white

c both counters are white.

[Grade A]

7 When Luella goes to work, she either goes by car or cycles.

The probability that she goes by car is $\frac{3}{5}$.

At lunchtime she either goes to the canteen or the gym.

The probability that she goes to the canteen is $\frac{4}{5}$.

a Draw a tree diagram to show her possible choices.

b Find the probability that:

   i she cycles and goes to the canteen

  ii she cycles or goes to the gym or does both.

[Grade A]

Revise 12.1 Formulae and simultaneous equations

Transforming more complicated formulae

Changing the subject of a formula is similar to solving an equation.

The new subject must appear on the left-hand side.

Work towards this, one step at a time.

If the new subject letter appears on both sides of the formula, first collect terms containing that letter on one side of the formula, as shown in the second worked example.

Simultaneous equations

There are two methods for solving **simultaneous equations**: elimination and substitution.

Solving by elimination

You need matching coefficients in order to eliminate one of the variables.

For example, if you add these equations:

$$7x + 2y = 3$$
$$3x - 2y = 7$$

you eliminate y, and have the equation: $10x = 10$

which tells you that: $x = 1$

> **The rule is:**
>
> **Signs Same Subtract**
>
> **Signs Difference Add**

Substitute this value for x in the first equation:

$$7 + 2y = 3$$
$$2y = -4$$
$$y = -2$$

You may have to multiply one or both of the equations to get matching coefficients, as shown in the worked example.

Solving by substitution

Rearrange one of the equations to make x or y the subject.

Then substitute the expression for this variable in the second equation.

For example, given these equations:

$$x + 3y = 5$$
$$3x + 8y = 12$$

make x the subject of the first equation: $x = 5 - 3y$

and substitute this in the second equation: $3(5 - 3y) + 8y = 12$

$$15 - 9y + 8y = 12$$
$$15 - y = 12$$
$$y = 3$$

> **Exam tip**
>
> Don't forget to find the values of both the unknowns when you solve a pair of simultaneous equations.

Substitute this value for y in the expression for x:

$$x = 5 - 9 = -4$$

The solution is: $x = -4, y = 3$.

Worked examples

The radius of a sphere $\quad\boxed{\text{C}}$

The formula for the surface area of a sphere is $A = 4\pi r^2$, where r is the radius of the sphere.

Make r the subject of the formula.

Solution

Start by changing over the sides of the equation to get r on the left-hand side:

$$4\pi r^2 = A$$

Divide both sides by 4π to get r^2 on its own:

$$r^2 = \frac{A}{4\pi}$$

Take the square root of both sides:

$$r = \sqrt{\frac{A}{4\pi}}$$

Subject is on both sides of the equation

A

Make x the subject of the formula: $4x - y = a(x - 5y)$.

Solution

Collect the terms that include x on one side of the formula:

$$4x - y = a(x - 5y)$$

$$4x - y = ax - 5ay \quad \longleftarrow \quad \boxed{\text{Multiply out the brackets.}}$$

$$4x - y + y = ax - 5ay + y \quad \longleftarrow \quad \boxed{\text{Add } y \text{ to both sides.}}$$

$$4x - ax = ax - 5ay + y - ax \quad \longleftarrow \quad \boxed{\text{Subtract } ax \text{ from both sides.}}$$

$$4x - ax = -5ay + y$$

$$x(4 - a) = y(1 - 5a) \quad \longleftarrow \quad \boxed{\text{Factorise both sides.}}$$

$$x = \frac{y(1 - 5a)}{(4 - a)} \quad \longleftarrow \quad \boxed{\text{Divide both sides by } (4 - a).}$$

Simultaneous equations

C

Solve the simultaneous equations:

$$2p - 3q = 13$$

$$5p - 2q = 16$$

Solution

There are no matching coefficients so you have to multiply the equations.

Multiply the first equation by 2 and the second equation by 3 to get $-6q$ in both equations:

$$4p - 6q = 26$$

$$15p - 6q = 48$$

Follow the rule 'Signs Same Subtract':

$$11p = 22 \quad \longleftarrow \quad \boxed{\text{Subtract first equation from second equation.}}$$

$$p = 2$$

Substitute $p = 2$ in the first equation:

$$4 - 3q = 13$$

$$-3q = 9$$

$$q = -3$$

Solution is: $p = 2$, $q = -3$. $\quad \longleftarrow \quad \boxed{\begin{array}{l}\text{Check by substituting in the second equation:} \\ (5 \times 2) - (2 \times -3) = 10 - -6 = 16 \quad \checkmark\end{array}}$

Revise 12.2 Inequalities and linear programming

Inequalities

There are four **inequality** symbols:

$<$	$\leqslant$	$>$	$\geqslant$
Less than	Less than or equal to	Greater than	Greater than or equal to

To solve an inequality (or **inequation**), take the same steps as you would to solve an equation.

Equation: $3x - 7 = 17$ Inequality: $3x - 7 < 17$

$$3x = 24 \qquad\qquad\qquad\qquad 3x < 24$$

$$x = 8 \qquad\qquad\qquad\qquad\quad x < 8$$

There is one very important difference between solving an inequality and solving an equation.

If you multiply or divide both sides of an inequality by a negative number, the inequality is reversed.

      $4 < 5$ but $-4 > -5$

so if $a < b$ then $-a > -b$

> **Exam tip**
>
> - Do *not* replace the inequality sign with an equals sign.
> - Make sure your answer includes the correct inequality sign.

Inequalities on a graph

You can represent an inequality, such as $x + y \geqslant 5$, as a **region** on a graph.

The **boundary** of this region will be the line $x + y = 5$.

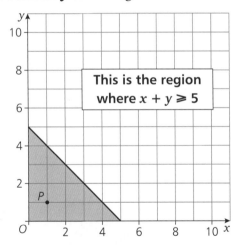

This is the region where $x + y \geqslant 5$

> **Exam tip**
>
> - You must show clearly which part of your graph is the required region.
> - It is a good idea to mark the region with the letter R.

The inequality $x + y \geqslant 5$ is called an included inequality because values include $x + y = 5$.

The boundary of an included inequality is shown by a solid line.

Note: $x + y > 5$ is called a strict inequality. The boundary of a strict inequality is shown by a broken line.

Which side of the boundary represents the inequality?

Pick a point such as $(0, 0)$, $(1, 0)$ or $(0, 1)$ and check whether it satisfies the inequality.

For example, $P(1, 1)$ does *not* satisfy $x + y \geqslant 5$, so this point is *not* in the region.

Linear programming

You can use inequalities represented by regions on a graph to solve practical problems.

You have to write down inequalities that express the limits of the problem.

For example: 'x men and y women are seated on a bus that has 36 seats.'

This tells us that: $x + y \leqslant 36$.

'There are at least twice as many women as men on the bus.'

This tells us that: $y \geqslant 2x$.

Worked examples

Solving inequalities

B

Solve the inequality: $7 - 3x > 5(x + 3)$.

Solution

$$7 - 3x > 5x + 15$$ ⟵   Multiply out the bracket.

$$-3x > 5x + 8$$ ⟵   Subtract 7 from both sides.

$$-8x > 8$$ ⟵   Subtract $5x$ from both sides.

$$-x > 1$$ ⟵   Divide both sides by 8.

$$x < -1$$ ⟵   Multiply both sides by -1.

Using inequalities to define a region

B

a   Show the region bounded by these inequalities: $x > 2$, $y > 1$ and $x + 2y \leqslant 8$.

b   Write down all the pairs of integer values that satisfy these inequalities.

Solution

a   The lines $x = 2$ and $y = 1$ are the boundaries of strict inequalities. They must be drawn with broken lines.

The line $x + 2y = 8$ is the boundary of an included inequality. It must be drawn with a solid line.

Shade out the regions which do *not* satisfy each inequality.

The triangular region marked R is the region that satisfies all three inequalities.

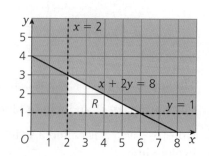

b   The points with integer values in the region are (3, 2) and (4, 2).
The pairs of integer values that satisfy these inequalities are $x = 3$, $y = 2$ and $x = 4$, $y = 2$.

Revise 12.3 Further algebra

Multiplying two brackets

Each term in one bracket has to be multiplied by each term in the other bracket.

Using a grid

Multiply out: $(2x - 5)(2x - 1)$.

×	$2x$	-5
$2x$	$4x^2$	$-10x$
-1	$-2x$	$+5$

$$(2x - 5)(2x - 1) = 4x^2 - 12x + 5$$

Using FOIL

Multiply out: $(y + 3)(3y - 2)$.

First terms: $(y + 3)(3y - 2)$ $y \times 3y = 3y^2$

Outer terms: $(y + 3)(3y - 2)$ $y \times -2 = -2y$

Inner terms: $(y + 3)(3y - 2)$ $+3 \times 3y = +9y$

Last terms: $(y + 3)(3y - 2)$ $+3 \times -2 = -6$

$$(y + 3)(3y - 2) = 3y^2 + 7y - 6$$

Separating out the first bracket

Multiply out: $(z - 4)(5z - 3)$.

$$(z - 4)(5z - 3) \rightarrow z(5z - 3) - 4(5z - 3)$$
$$= 5z^2 - 3z - 20z + 12$$
$$= 5z^2 - 23z + 12$$

> **Exam tip**
>
> Remember that each sign belongs to the term that follows it.

Factorising quadratic expressions

This process is the opposite of multiplying out two brackets.

$$x^2 + 3x - 40 = (\ \ ?\ \ )(\ \ ?\ \ )$$

Using the **F** of FOIL, the first terms must be x and x.

Using the **L** of FOIL, the last terms must multiply together to give -40.

Possible factors of -40 are:

$$-1 \text{ and } +40,\ +1 \text{ and } -40,$$
$$-2 \text{ and } +20,\ +2 \text{ and } -20,$$
$$-4 \text{ and } +10,\ +4 \text{ and } -10,$$
$$-5 \text{ and } +8,\ \ +5 \text{ and } -8.$$

The **I**nner and **O**uter terms have to combine to get $+3x$.
The only factors that combine to give $+3$ are -5 and $+8$.

The solution is: $x^2 + 3x - 40 = (x - 5)(x + 8)$

> **Exam tip**
>
> - The brackets should always contain integers, not fractions or decimals.
> - Check your answer by multiplying out the brackets to see if you get the original quadratic expression.

The difference of squares

The factors of $p^2 - q^2$ are $(p - q)(p + q)$.

For example:

$$x^2 - 49 = (x - 7)(x + 7)$$

$$25 - 4y^2 = (5 - 2y)(5 + 2y)$$

Harder quadratics

When the coefficient of x^2 is not 1, there are more possible factors to consider.

For example:

$$3x^2 - x - 14 = (3x \dots)(x \dots)$$

The last terms in the brackets must multiply to -14.

Possible factors of -14 are:

$$-1 \text{ and } +14, \ +1 \text{and} -14,$$

$$-2 \text{ and } +7, \ +2 \text{ and } -7.$$

You have to decide which factor of -14 goes in the bracket with $3x$ and which goes with x to give the middle term of $-x$.

The solution is:

$$3x^2 - x - 14 = (3x - 7)(x + 2)$$

Four-term expressions

To factorise a four-term expression, look at the terms in pairs to find a common factor.

For example:

$$x^2 - 5x - xy + 5y$$

can be split into $x^2 - 5x$, which factorises to $x(x - 5)$

and $-xy + 5y$, which factorises to $-y(x - 5)$.

So $\quad x^2 - 5x - xy + 5y = x(x - 5) - y(x - 5)$

$$= (x - y)(x - 5)$$

> **Exam tip**
>
> - Find a factor for one pair of terms.
> - You should then expect to find the same factor in the other pair.

You may have to rearrange the terms before you can find the common factors.

Algebraic fractions

Addition and subtraction

Use common denominators for addition and subtraction.

For example:

$$\frac{x}{3} + \frac{x}{4} = \frac{4x}{12} + \frac{3x}{12}$$

$$= \frac{7x}{12}$$

Dividing by a common factor

An algebraic fraction can be simplified by dividing the numerator and the denominator by a common factor.

For example:

$$\frac{4xy}{6y} = \frac{2x}{3}$$

After dividing numerator and denominator by the common factor $2y$.

and

$$\frac{25 - y^2}{15 - 8y + y^2} = \frac{{}^1(5 - y)(5 + y)}{{}_1(5 - y)(3 - y)}$$

$$= \frac{(5 + y)}{(3 - y)}$$

> **Exam tip**
>
> If you are told to simplify an algebraic fraction, you should expect to find a common factor.

Solving quadratic equations

By factorisation

If $a \times b = 0$, then either a or b (or both of them) must be 0.

To solve the quadratic equation $2x^2 + 5x - 7 = 0$, first factorise to get $(x - 1)(2x + 7) = 0$.

If $(x - 1)(2x + 7) = 0$, then either $(x - 1) = 0$ or $(2x + 7) = 0$

$(x - 1) = 0$ leads to $x = 1$, and $(2x + 7) = 0$ leads to $x = -3.5$

Check your answer by substitution:	$2 \times 1^2 + (5 \times 1) - 7 = 2 + 5 - 7 = 0$ ✓
	$2 \times (-3.5)^2 + (5 \times -3.5) - 7 = 24.5 - 17.5 - 7 = 0$ ✓

Some quadratics cannot be factorised. Instead you have to use other methods.

By completing the square

Some quadratic equations are perfect squares.

For example:

$$x^2 - 10x + 25 = (x - 5)^2$$

The number in the bracket (-5) is half the coefficient of x (-10).

You can rearrange any quadratic to include a perfect square.

For example:

$$x^2 - 10x + 14 = x^2 - 10x + 25 - 11$$

$$= (x - 5)^2 - 11$$

This is called 'completing the square'.

Using the formula

The formula $x = \dfrac{-b \pm \sqrt{b^2 - 4ac}}{2a}$ can be used to solve the

quadratic equation $ax^2 + bx + c = 0$.

> Make sure the quadratic equation is in this form before you start to write down values for a, b and c.

The second worked example shows how to use the formula.

> **Exam tip**
>
> - If you are told to give your answers correct to 1 or 2 decimal places, you have to use the formula.
> - If you are trying to find the square root of a negative number, go back and check your working. There is no square root of a negative number.

Worked examples

Algebraic fractions

A*

Simplify: $\dfrac{3}{x-2} - \dfrac{2}{x-3}$

Solution

Put a bracket around each denominator:

$$\frac{3}{(x-2)} - \frac{2}{(x-3)}$$

The common denominator is $(x-2)(x-3)$:

$$\frac{3}{(x-2)} - \frac{2}{(x-3)} = \frac{3(x-3)}{(x-2)(x-3)} - \frac{2(x-2)}{(x-3)(x-2)}$$

$$= \frac{3x - 9 - 2x + 4}{(x-2)(x-3)} \quad\longleftarrow \boxed{-2 \times -2 = +4}$$

$$= \frac{x-5}{(x-2)(x-3)}$$

Solving a quadratic equation by the formula

A

Solve the equation: $3x^2 - 5x - 4 = 0$, giving your answers correct to 2 decimal places.

Solution

Start by writing down the values of a, b and c. $\longleftarrow$ $\boxed{\text{Make sure you include their signs.}}$

$$a = 3, b = -5, c = -4$$

Substitute into the formula.

Start by working out the value of $b^2 - 4ac$ $\longleftarrow$ $\boxed{\text{Be very careful with the negative signs.}}$

$$b^2 - 4ac = (-5)^2 - 4 \times 3 \times (-4)$$

$$= 25 + 48 = 73$$

$$x = \frac{--5 \pm \sqrt{73}}{2 \times 3}$$

$$= \frac{5 \pm 8.544\ldots}{6}$$

$$= \frac{5 + 8.544\ldots}{6} \text{ or } \frac{5 - 8.544\ldots}{6}$$

$$= \frac{13.544\ldots}{6} \text{ or } \frac{-3.544\ldots}{6}$$

$$= 2.257\ldots \text{ or } -0.590\ldots$$

Solution: $x = 2.26$ or -0.59 (to 2 d.p.)

Practise 12.1 – 12.3

1 Make r the subject of the formula $V = \pi r^2 h$.

[Grade C]

2 Solve these inequalities:

  a $3x - 2 \geqslant 16$

  b $y + 7 < 11 + 5y$

[Grades C–B]

3 Find the coordinates of the point of intersection of the straight lines:

    $4x + y = 5$

    $2x - 5y = 8$

[Grade C]

4

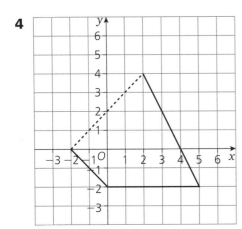

The area inside this quadrilateral is defined by four inequalities.

One of these is $x + y \geqslant -2$.

Write down the other three inequalities.

[Grade B]

5 There are x adults and y children on a theme park boat trip.

The boat can carry a maximum of 14 passengers.

  a Use this information to write down an inequality in x and y.

The owner of the boat will not run the trip unless he has at least 9 passengers.

  b Write down another inequality.

Weight restrictions limit the number of adults on the boat to 8.

  c Write down another inequality.

For safety, there has to be at least one adult on the boat for every 2 children.

  d Write down another inequality.

  e Show all your inequalities on a graph and mark clearly the region where values of x and y must lie.

[Grades C–A]

6 Multiply out and simplify:

    a $(p + 8)(p - 8)$

    b $(4q - 3)(q + 2)$

                                                            [Grade B]

7 Factorise:

    a $m^2 + 8m + 7$

    b $n^2 - n - 6$

    c $5t^2 + 3t - 2$

    d $pq - 2p - 10 + 5q$

                                                        [Grades B–A]

8 Factorise completely:

    a $3x^2 - 3$

    b $2y^2 - 12y + 18$

    [Hint: Take out a single term factor first, then factorise into two brackets.]

                                                          [Grade A]

9 Simplify:

    a $\dfrac{3}{2x} - \dfrac{2}{5x}$

    b $\dfrac{y^2 - 5y + 4}{2y^2 - 7y - 4}$

                                                          [Grade A]

10 a Solve the equation $2x^2 + 7x - 15 = 0$.

    b The quadratic expression $y^2 + 18y - 2$ can be written in the form $(y + a)^2 - b$.

       Find the values of a and b.

    c Solve the equation $4m^2 + m - 1 = 0$, giving your answers correct to two decimal places.

                                                          [Grade A]

13 Trigonometry

Learning outcomes

After this chapter you should be able to:

- apply Pythagoras' theorem   C

- apply the sine, cosine and tangent ratios for acute angles to the calculation of a side or an angle of a right-angled triangle   C

- interpret and use three-figure bearings measured clockwise from the North (i.e. 000°–360°)   D C

- solve problems involving angles of elevation and depression   C

- extend sine and cosine values to angles between 90° and 180°, and use the sine and cosine rules for any triangle   A

- use the trigonometrical formula for the area of a triangle   A

- solve simple trigonometrical problems in three dimensions.   A A*

Revise 13.1 Trigonometry

Pythagoras' theorem

The longest side of a right-angled triangle is always opposite the right angle. It is called the **hypotenuse**.

If the shorter sides of a right angled-triangle are **a** and **b**, and the hypotenuse is **c**, then Pythagoras' theorem states that:

$$a^2 + b^2 = c^2$$

You can split rectangles and isosceles triangles into two right-angled triangles.

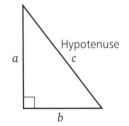

Exam tip

Pythagoras' theorem only works for right-angled triangles.

Length of a line segment

You can use Pythagoras' theorem to find the length of a line segment. The second worked example shows how to do this.

Trigonometry

The study of right-angled triangles is called **trigonometry**.

A right-angled triangle has a **hypotenuse**.

The two shorter sides are named according to their position.

In the diagram, the base is opposite to the angle $x°$, and so it is called the **opposite side**.

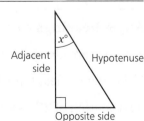

The third side is called the **adjacent side**, because it is adjacent to, or next to, the angle of $x°$.

The **sine** of $x° = \dfrac{\text{opposite side}}{\text{hypotenuse}}$

The **cosine** of $x° = \dfrac{\text{adjacent side}}{\text{hypotenuse}}$

The **tangent** of $x° = \dfrac{\text{opposite side}}{\text{adjacent side}}$

These are usually abbreviated to the first three letters, so you write:

$$\sin x = \frac{\text{opp}}{\text{hyp}} \qquad \cos x = \frac{\text{adj}}{\text{hyp}} \qquad \tan x = \frac{\text{opp}}{\text{adj}}$$

The values of sine, cosine and tangent for any angle can be obtained from your calculator.

Pressing the keys ⟨sin⟩ ⟨7⟩ ⟨2⟩ ⟨=⟩ gives an answer of 0.95105651…

This is the sine of an angle of 72°.

Pressing the keys ⟨inv⟩ ⟨cos⟩ ⟨0⟩ ⟨.⟩ ⟨6⟩ ⟨0⟩ ⟨1⟩ ⟨8⟩ gives an answer of 53.0010…

This tells you that the angle of 53.0010° has a cosine of 0.6018

This can be written as: $\cos^{-1} 0.6018 = 53.0010…°$

> ### Exam tip
>
> You must learn these three formulae.
>
> You can remember these by learning the word SOHCAHTOA.
>
> Or use a mnemonic such as 'Some Old Hairy Camels Are Hairier Than Others Are'.

> ### Exam tip
>
> To do these calculations your calculator must be in 'degree' mode. Check that a small 'd' or 'deg' is showing on the display.

Angles of elevation and depression

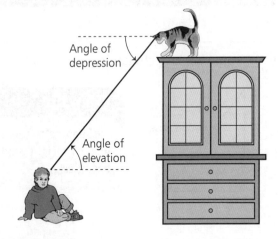

When you look up from the horizontal, you look through an **angle of elevation**.

If you look down, the angle between the horizontal and the line of sight is an **angle of depression**.

Bearings

Angle bearings are measured clockwise, from North.

Bearings are always written as 3-figure bearings.

If the angle is less than 100°, write a 0 before it.

So a bearing of 27° is written as 027°.

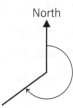

North

Worked examples

Height and area of an isosceles triangle

C

An isosceles triangle has two sides of 12 cm and one of 8 cm.

Calculate:

a the perpendicular height of the triangle

b the area of the triangle.

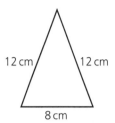

Solution

a Draw the perpendicular height which bisects the base of the triangle. Then use Pythagoras' theorem on one of the right-angled triangles.

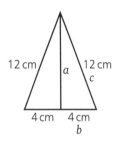

In the right-hand triangle:

$a^2 + b^2 = c^2$

$a^2 + 4^2 = 12^2$

$a^2 + 16 = 144$

$a^2 = 128$

$a = \sqrt{128} = 11.313708\ldots$ cm $= 11.3$ cm (to 1 d.p.)

b Area $= \frac{1}{2} \times$ base $\times$ height $= \frac{1}{2} \times 8 \times 11.313708\ldots = 45.3$ cm^2 (to 1 d.p.)

Exam tip

Avoid rounding until the end of the calculation.

Finding the length of a line segment

B

$A(4, -1)$ and $B(-2, -3)$ are the endpoints of a line segment.

Find the length of AB.

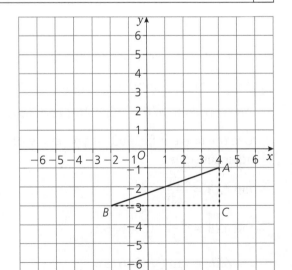

Solution

Draw in the triangle ABC.

AB is the hypotenuse of this triangle.

$AB^2 = AC^2 + BC^2$

$\quad = (-1 - -3)^2 + (4 - -2)^2$

$\quad = 4 + 36 = 40$

$AB = \sqrt{40} = 2\sqrt{10} = 6.3$ units (to 1 d.p.)

Finding a length and angle of elevation

A vertical pole *AB* of length 11 m is held in place by a rope *AC* as shown.

C is 8 m from the foot of the pole.

The angle between the ground and the rope is 67°.

A point *X* is 13 m from the foot of the pole.

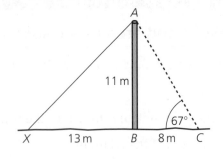

Calculate:

a the length of the rope

b the angle of elevation of the top of the pole at *X*.

Solution

a First, label the sides of triangle *ABC* opp, adj and hyp on the diagram.

AC is the hypotenuse as it is opposite to the right angle.

AB is opposite to the angle of 67° and *BC* is adjacent to it.

You know the length of the opposite side and need to find the length of *AC*, the hypotenuse.

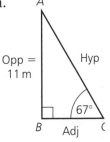

The sine formula contains the opposite side and the hypotenuse.

$$\sin 67° = \frac{\text{opp}}{\text{hyp}}$$

$$\sin 67° = \frac{11}{AC}$$

$$\sin 67° \times AC = 11$$

$$AC = \frac{11}{\sin 67°}$$

$$AC = 11.9 \text{ m (to 1 d.p.)}$$

b First, label the sides of triangle *AXB* opp, adj and hyp on the diagram.

AX is the hypotenuse as it is opposite to the right angle.

AB is opposite to the angle *AXB* and *BX* is adjacent to it.

Use the tangent formula as you know the opposite and adjacent sides.

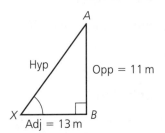

$$\tan AXB = \frac{\text{opp}}{\text{adj}}$$

$$\tan AXB = \frac{11}{13} = 0.84615...$$

$$AXB = \tan^{-1} 0.84615...$$

$$AXB = 40.2° \text{(to 1 d.p.)}$$

Finding a bearing

c

Three towns, A, B and C are situated so that B is 11 km due East of A, and C is 23 km due South of B.

Calculate the bearing of C from A.

Solution

Draw a diagram.

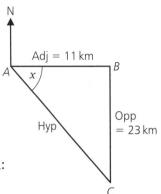

You need to calculate angle x.

You know the opposite side and the adjacent side, so use tangent formula:

$$\tan x = \frac{\text{opp}}{\text{adj}}$$

$$\tan x = \frac{23}{11} = 2.090909\ldots$$

$$x = \tan^{-1} 2.090909\ldots = 64.4° \text{ (to 1 d.p.)}$$

The bearing of C from A is angle $NAC = 90° + 64.4° = 154.4°$

Exam tip

- Always draw and label a diagram.
- Always write down the appropriate formula for sin, cos or tan.
- Make sure you know how to use your calculator to find an angle from the sin, cos or tan by using the $\sin^{-1}$, $\cos^{-1}$ or $\tan^{-1}$ keys.

Revise 13.2 Trigonometry rules

Angles greater than 90 degrees

This is the graph of $y = \sin x°$.

It shows that $\sin x° = \sin (180 - x)°$.

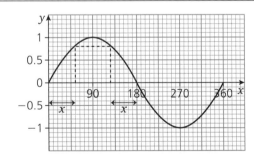

This is the graph of $y = \cos x°$.

It shows that $\cos x° = -\cos (180 - x)°$.

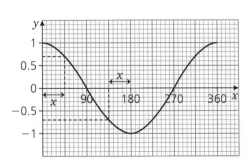

In triangle ABC, side a is opposite to angle A, side b is opposite to angle B and side c is opposite to angle C.

Then **sine rule** states that: $\dfrac{a}{\sin A} = \dfrac{b}{\sin B} = \dfrac{c}{\sin C}$

It can also be written as: $\dfrac{\sin A}{a} = \dfrac{\sin B}{b} = \dfrac{\sin C}{c}$

The **cosine rule** states that: $a^2 = b^2 + c^2 - 2bc \cos A$.

It can also be written as: $\qquad b^2 = a^2 + c^2 - 2ac \cos B$ (by replacing A with B, a with b and b with a)

or $\qquad\qquad\qquad c^2 = b^2 + a^2 - 2ba \cos C$ (by replacing A with C, a with c and c with a).

Using trigonometry, the area of a triangle can be calculated as:

$\qquad$ **Area** $= \frac{1}{2}ab \sin C$

It is also equal to $\frac{1}{2}ac \sin B$ and $\frac{1}{2}bc \sin A$.

Three dimensions

Trigonometry can be used in three dimensions.

You need to be able to identify right-angled triangles. See the second worked example.

Worked examples

Applying the sine rule and cosine rule

[A]

$ABCD$ is a quadrilateral.

$AB = 9.2$ cm, $AD = 6.8$ cm, angle $BAD = 80°$, angle $BCD = 54°$ and angle $DBC = 72°$.

Calculate: **a** BD $\qquad$ **b** CD.

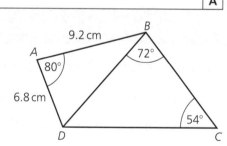

Solution

a In triangle ABD, you know the length of two sides and need to calculate the third length. You know the size of one angle.

The cosine rule contains three sides and one angle.

You know angle A, so use

$a^2 = b^2 + c^2 - 2bc \cos A$

As the vertices are A, B and D, you replace c with d:

$a^2 = b^2 + d^2 - 2bd \cos A$

$a^2 = 6.8^2 + 9.2^2 - 2 \times 6.8 \times 9.2 \times \cos 80°$

$a^2 = 46.24 + 84.64 - 21.72685999\ldots$

$a = \sqrt{109.15314\ldots} = 10.4$ cm (to 1 d.p.)

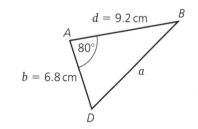

b In triangle *BCD*, you know two angles and the length of one side. You need to calculate another length.

The sine rule uses two angles and two lengths.

The angles are *B* and *C* and the sides are *b* and *c*.

To find a side, write the formula with the sides on top:

$$\frac{b}{\sin B} = \frac{c}{\sin C}$$

$$\frac{b}{\sin 72°} = \frac{10.4}{\sin 54°}$$

$$\frac{b}{\sin 72°} = 12.85510696...$$

$$b = 12.85510696... \times \sin 72° = 12.2\,\text{cm (to 1 d.p.)}$$

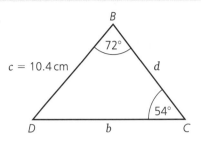

Finding the height of a 3-D object

[A]

A tripod has three legs *AB*, *AC* and *AD* of length 1.9 m.

The feet form an equilateral triangle *BCD* with sides of 0.7 m.

Calculate *AX*, the height of the tripod.

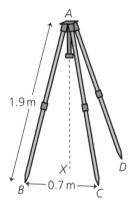

Solution

Draw a sketch of the equilateral triangle *BCD*.

BXC is an isosceles triangle. *XM* is the perpendicular bisector of *BC*.

In triangle *BXM*,

$$\cos 30° = \frac{BM}{BX}$$

$$BX = \frac{BM}{\cos 30°} = \frac{0.35}{0.866...} = 0.404\,\text{m (to the nearest mm)}$$

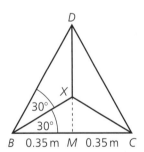

Draw triangle *ABX*.

Using Pythagoras' theorem:

$$BX^2 + AX^2 = AB^2$$

$$AX^2 = 1.9^2 - 0.404^2$$

$$AX^2 = 3.446784$$

$$AX = \sqrt{3.446784} = 1.86\,\text{m (to the nearest cm)}$$

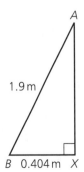

Practise 13.1 – 13.2

1 An isosceles triangle *ABC* has *AB* = *AC* = 11 cm and *BC* = 9 cm.

Calculate angle *ABC*.

[Grade C]

2 The quadrilateral *ABCD* has *AB* = 9.7 cm,
CD = 3.2 cm, *AD* = 20 cm,
angle *BAD* = 67° and angle *ADC* = 90°.

Calculate angle *BCD*.

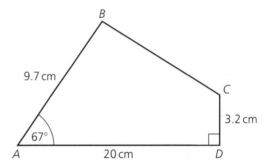

[Grade B]

3 The diagram shows a ramp.

CD = 6 m and *BC* = 4.5 m

Angle *BED* = 35°

BE is a diagonal stripe painted on the ramp.

Calculate:

a angle *BDC* **b** the length of *DE*.

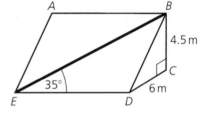

[Grade B]

4 In triangle *ABC*, *AB* = 8.6 cm, *AC* = 9.7 cm
and angle *BAC* = 61°.

Calculate:

a the length of *BC*

b the size of angle *ABC*.

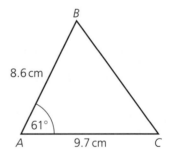

[Grade A]

5 *B* is 9.2 km from *A* on a bearing of 058°.
C is 14.3 km from *B*.
The bearing of *C* from *B* is 160°.

Calculate:

a angle *ABC*

b the distance from *A* to *C*

c the bearing of *C* from *A*.

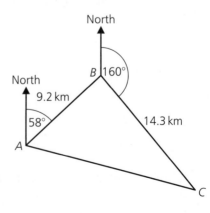

[Grade A]

6 A tetrahedron has four faces that are all equilateral triangles. The sides are all 12 cm.

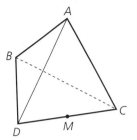

 a Calculate the surface area of the tetrahedron.

 b If *M* is the midpoint of *CD*, calculate:

 i the length of *BM*

 ii the angle *ABM*.

[Grade A]

Practice exam questions: Paper 1

1     $A(-6, -4)$ and $B(3, -2)$ are 2 points.

Find the midpoint of AB.   *(2 marks)*

2   A square has side 5.7 cm correct to the nearest millimetre.

Calculate the lower bound of the area of the square.

Write down all the figures on your calculator.   *(2 marks)*

3   Write down the number of

    a   lines of symmetry of a rectangle   *(1 mark)*

    b   planes of symmetry of a cuboid with the length, width and height all different.   *(1 mark)*

4

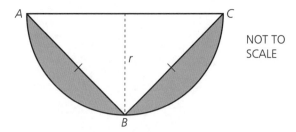

NOT TO SCALE

A triangle ABC is inside a semicircle, radius r. $AB = BC$.

Write down an expression, in its simplest form, for the shaded area.   *(2 marks)*

5   Evaluate $49^{\frac{1}{2}} \times 64^{\frac{2}{3}}$.   *(2 marks)*

6     $\mathbf{A} = \begin{pmatrix} 2 & 3 \\ -4 & 1 \end{pmatrix}$

Find $\mathbf{A}^{-1}$, the inverse of $\mathbf{A}$.   *(2 marks)*

7   Factorise $f^2 - 25g^2$.   *(2 marks)*

8   W is inversely proportional to the square of x.

When $x = 5$, $W = 10.2$.

Find the value of W when $x = 3$.   *(3 marks)*

9 Without using a calculator and showing all working, work out the value of

$\dfrac{-\frac{1}{4} - \frac{4}{9}}{\frac{1}{4} \times \frac{4}{9}}$. Give your answer as a mixed number in its simplest form. *(3 marks)*

10 Solve the inequality $3(4x - 2) - 2(5x - 8) \leqslant 0$ *(3 marks)*

11 $x^2 - 3x + 5$ can be written in the form $(x + p)^2 + q$.

Find the values of p and q. *(3 marks)*

12 The scale of a map is 1 cm represents $\frac{1}{2}$ km.

Find

  a the actual distance apart, in km, of 2 places which are 3.5 cm apart on the map *(1 mark)*

  b the actual area, in km², of a region that is 12.4 cm² on the map. *(2 marks)*

13 Work out $\dfrac{2.65 \times 10^{-3}}{4.78 \times 10^{3}}$.

Give your answer in standard form, correct to 2 significant figures. *(3 marks)*

14 Solve the simultaneous equations

$$\frac{3}{4}x - 2y = 12$$
$$6x + 11y = 15$$ *(4 marks)*

15 $\mathscr{E} = \{x : 0 < x < 20\}$

$\mathbf{P} = \{x : x \text{ is a prime number}\}$

$\mathbf{M} = \{x : x \text{ is a multiple of } 4\}$

$\mathbf{C} = \{x : x \text{ is a factor of } 24\}$

  a In the Venn diagram, write in the correct place

    i 8

    ii 13.

  b Complete

    i $\mathbf{P} \cap \mathbf{M} =$ *(1 mark)*

    ii $n(\mathbf{P} \cap \mathbf{C}) =$ *(1 mark)*

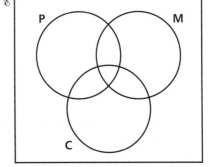

(1 mark)

(1 mark)

16

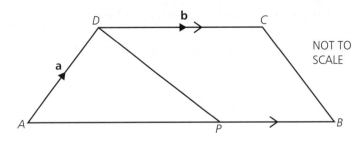

ABCD is a trapezium. **AD** = **a**, **DC** = **b** and *AB* = 2 × *DC*.

a Find, in terms of **a** and **b**

   i **AC** *(1 mark)*

   ii **CB**. *(1 mark)*

b *P* is a point on *AB* such that *AP* : *PB* = 3 : 2.

   Find **DP** in terms of **a** and **b**. *(2 marks)*

17 $y = 2 + \dfrac{3}{x - 2}$

Rearrange the formula to make *x* the subject. *(4 marks)*

18 The shaded region is defined by 5 inequalities.

One of the inequalities is $y \geq -\frac{1}{2}x - 1$.

Find and write down the other 4 inequalities.

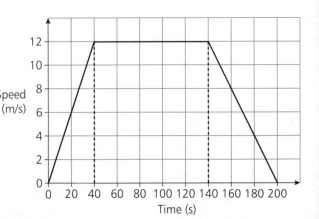

(4 marks)

19 The graph shows the journey of a metro train between two stations.

a Calculate the acceleration, in m/s², during the first 40 seconds. *(1 mark)*

b Calculate the distance, in metres, between the two stations. *(3 marks)*

c Find the average speed, in metres/second, for the whole journey. *(1 mark)*

20   *A, B, C* and *D* are points on the circumference of a circle, centre *O*.

DA = DC and angle *AOC* = 112°.

Calculate

a *x*   *(1 mark)*

b *y*   *(1 mark)*

c *z*.   *(3 marks)*

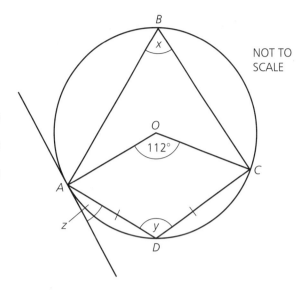

NOT TO SCALE

21   A bag contains 14 red balls and 11 blue balls.

A ball is taken at random from the bag and is not replaced.

Another ball is then taken at random from the bag.

a If the first ball taken is red, explain why the probability that the second ball taken is also red is $\frac{13}{24}$.   *(1 mark)*

b

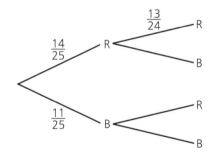

Complete the tree diagram by adding the 3 remaining probabilities.   *(3 marks)*

c Find the probability that at least one red ball is taken.   *(3 marks)*

Practice exam questions: Paper 2

1   **a**   A car dealer advertised a car for $8800.

    i   In a sale the price was reduced by 20%.

      Show that the cost in the sale was $7040. *(1 mark)*

    ii   The advertised $8800 was 60% more than the dealer paid for the car.

      Calculate how much the dealer paid for the car. *(3 marks)*

  b   Josh bought the car for $7040. He paid a deposit and borrowed the remainder.

    i   The ratio, Deposit : Remainder = 3 : 13

      Calculate the remainder. *(2 marks)*

    ii   He borrowed the remainder at 4.5% compound interest and repaid the full amount at the end of three years.

      Calculate the amount he repaid. Give your answer to the nearest dollar. *(4 marks)*

2   The table shows the marks out of 100 gained by 80 students in a mathematics exam.

$0 < x \leqslant 10$	$10 < x \leqslant 20$	$20 < x \leqslant 30$	$30 < x \leqslant 40$	$40 < x \leqslant 50$
0	9	10	12	15

$50 < x \leqslant 60$	$60 < x \leqslant 70$	$70 < x \leqslant 80$	$80 < x \leqslant 90$	$90 < x \leqslant 100$
16	8	6	3	1

  a   Write down the modal interval. *(1 mark)*

  b   Calculate an estimate of the mean. *(4 marks)*

  c   Make a cumulative frequency table for the data. *(2 marks)*

  d   Using a scale of 2 cm for 10 marks on the horizontal axis and 2 cm for 10 students on the vertical axis, draw the cumulative frequency graph. *(4 marks)*

  e   Use your cumulative frequency graph to find an estimate of

    i   the median *(1 mark)*

    ii   the 30th percentile *(1 mark)*

    iii   the number of students gaining more than 65 marks. *(2 marks)*

  f   A different frequency table is made for the results.

$0 < x \leqslant 30$	$30 < x \leqslant 40$	$40 < x \leqslant 80$	$80 < x \leqslant 100$
19	12	45	4

  A histogram is drawn to represent the data in this table.

  The height of the column for the interval $30 < x \leqslant 40$ is 8 cm.

  Calculate the heights of the other three columns. *(4 marks)*

3   The table shows some of the values of the function $f(x) = x^2 + \dfrac{2}{x}$, $x \neq 0$.

x	-3	-2	-1	-0.75	-0.4	0.4	0.75	1	2	3
y	8.3	3	-1	-2.1	p	5.2	3.2	q	5	r

a   Find the values of p, q and r, correct to 1 decimal place. *(3 marks)*

b   Draw the graph of $y = f(x)$ for $-3 \leqslant x \leqslant 3$.

Use a scale of 2 cm to 1 unit on the x axis, and 1 cm to 1 unit on the y axis. *(4 marks)*

c   By drawing a suitable straight line, find 3 values of x where

$$f(x) = x + 3$$ *(3 marks)*

d $x^2 + \dfrac{2}{x} = x + 3$ can be written as $x^3 + ax^2 + bx + c = 0$.

Find the values of a, b and c. *(3 marks)*

e   Draw a tangent to the graph of $y = f(x)$ at the point where $x = 1.5$.

Use it to estimate the gradient of $y = f(x)$ when $x = 1.5$. *(3 marks)*

4

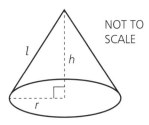

NOT TO SCALE

A cone has radius r, height h and slant height l.

a   When $r = 4.6\,\text{cm}$ and $h = 11.7\,\text{cm}$, show that $l = 12.57\,\text{cm}$ correct to 2 decimal places. *(2 marks)*

b   For a cone, the curved surface area is πrl and the volume is $\frac{1}{3}\pi r^2 h$.

For the cone in **part a**, calculate

  i   the curved surface area *(2 marks)*

  ii   the volume. *(2 marks)*

c   The cone in **part a** is an open cone.

The net of this cone is a sector of a circle. Calculate

  i   the perimeter *(3 marks)*

  ii   the angle of the sector. *(3 marks)*

d   Draw the net of this cone. *(1 mark)*

5

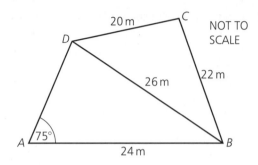

The quadrilateral, *ABCD*, represents a plot of land, with a path, *BD*, across it.

a   **i** Using a scale of 1 : 200, draw an accurate plan of the plot of land.   *(3 marks)*

     ii Measure and write down the sizes of angles *ADB* and *BCD*.   *(2 marks)*

    iii A second path is such that all points on it are equidistant from *AB* and *AD*.

       Using a straight edge and compasses only, construct this path.   *(2 marks)*

    iv A third path is such that all points on it are equidistant from *A* and *D*.

       Using a straight edge and compasses only, construct this path.   *(2 marks)*

     v Shade the region that is nearer to *AB* than to *AD* and is nearer to *A* than to *D*.   *(1 mark)*

b Using trigonometry and showing all your working, calculate

     i angle *ADB*   *(3 marks)*

    ii angle *BCD*   *(4 marks)*

    iii the area of *ABCD*.   *(3 marks)*

6   **a** Using a scale of 1 cm to 1 unit, draw *x* and *y* axes from -8 to 8.   *(1 mark)*

    b On the grid, plot the points $A(1, 1)$, $B(4, 3)$, $C(2, 4)$ and joint them to form a triangle.   *(1 mark)*

    c Draw the reflection of triangle *ABC* in the line $y = -x$.

       Label the image $A_1B_1C_1$.   *(2 marks)*

    d Rotate triangle $A_1B_1C_1$ through 90° anticlockwise about $(0, 0)$.

       Label the image $A_2B_2C_2$.   *(2 marks)*

    e Describe fully the single transformation which maps triangle *ABC* onto triangle $A_2B_2C_2$. *(2 marks)*

    f A transformation is represented by the matrix $\begin{pmatrix} -2 & 0 \\ 0 & 1 \end{pmatrix}$.

       i Draw the image of triangle *ABC* under this transformation.

         Label the image $A_3B_3C_3$.   *(3 marks)*

      ii Describe fully the single transformation represented by the matrix $\begin{pmatrix} -2 & 0 \\ 0 & 1 \end{pmatrix}$.   *(2 marks)*

    g Draw the image of triangle *ABC* under a shear, scale factor 1, invariant line the *x*-axis.

       Label the image *PQR*.   *(2 marks)*

7    $f(x) = 3x + 2$ $g(x) = \frac{4}{x} - 1$ $h(x) = 3^x$

    a   Find the value of $gf(6)$. *(1 mark)*

    b   Work out $gf(x)$ as a single fraction. *(2 marks)*

    c   Find $g^{-1}(x)$. *(2 marks)*

    d   Find $hh(2)$. *(2 marks)*

    e   Find the value of x when $h(x) = g\left(\frac{18}{5}\right)$. *(2 marks)*

8   The diagram shows a trapezium *ABCD* with perpendicular height *DE*.
$DC = x$, $AB = x + 4$, $DE = 2x - 1$ and Angle $DAE = 68°$.

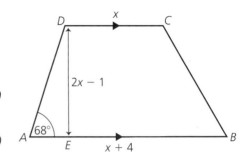

    a   Show that $2x^2 + 3x - 135 = 0$
       Make all your working clear. *(4 marks)*

    b   **i**   Solve the quadratic equation in **part a**. *(3 marks)*

       ii   Work out *ED*. *(2 marks)*

    c   Calculate *AD*. *(3 marks)*

9   The table shows some terms of several sequences.

Term	1	2	3	4		9	
Sequence **P**	8	5	2	−1		p	
Sequence **Q**	1	4	9	16		q	
Sequence **R**	$\frac{1}{3}$	$\frac{2}{5}$	$\frac{3}{7}$	$\frac{4}{9}$		r	
Sequence **S**	8	27	64	125		s	
Sequence **T**	1	4	16	64		t	
Sequence **U**	7	23	48	61		u	

    a   Find the values of p, q, r, s, t and u. *(6 marks)*

    b   Find the nth term of sequence

       i   **P** *(1 mark)*

       ii   **Q** *(1 mark)*

       iii   **R** *(1 mark)*

       iv   **S** *(1 mark)*

       v   **T** *(1 mark)*

       vi   **U**. *(1 mark)*

    c   Which term of sequence **P** is equal to −127? *(2 marks)*

    d   Which term in sequence **T** is equal to 4 194 304? *(2 marks)*

Answers

Practise 1.1 – 1.3

1 **a** Angle $BCD = 68°$ (interior angles add up to 180° since AB is parallel to DC)
Angle $CDA = 112°$ (interior angles add up to 180° since AD is parallel to BC)
Angle $DAB = 68°$ (interior angles add up to 180° since AB is parallel to DC)
Note: Other reasons are possible.

b **i** 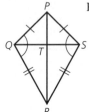 Kite **ii** Angle PSR
iii Triangle RQT

2 **a** **i** and **ii** 162° **b** 15 sides **c** 120°

3 **a** **i** 37° (angle sum of a triangle = 180°)
ii 53° (alternate angles are equal since PQ is parallel to ST)
iii 90° (vertically opposite angles are equal)
iv 37° (alternate angles are equal since PQ is parallel to ST)
Note: Other reasons are possible.

b $TS = 10$ cm because triangle PQR is **similar** to triangle TSR (since all angles are equal)

c 24 cm²

4 12 cm

5 **a** 18.0 cm (3 s.f.) **b** 14.1 cm (3 s.f.)

6 $a = 54°$ (angles subtended by the same arc)
$b = 108°$ (angle subtended at the centre is twice the angle subtended at the circumference)
$c = 90°$ (angle in a semicircle)
$d = 20°$ (angle sum of a triangle)
$e = 110°$ (opposite angles of a cyclic quadrilateral add up to 180°)
$f = 28°$ (angle between a tangent and radius is 90°)
$g = 62°$ (equal angles of isosceles triangle since tangents are equal in length)
$h = 56°$ (angle sum of a triangle with the other two angles both being 62°)
$i = 124°$ (equal radii give an isosceles triangle with the other two angles both being 28°)
Note: Other reasons are possible.

7 $p = 36°$ (alternate angles equal since AB is parallel to DC)
$q = 36°$ (angles subtended by the same arc BC)
$r = p = 36°$ (angles subtended by the same arc AD)
$s = 40°$ (angles subtended by the same arc CD)
$t = 68°$ (opposite angles of a cyclic quadrilateral add up to 180°)

$v = 66°$ (from angle sum of triangle OST with angle $OST = 90°$ since it lies between a tangent and radius)
$w = 33°$ (angle subtended at the circumference by arc SR is half of the angle at the centre)
$x = 57°$ (since $w + x$ = angle in a semicircle = 90°)
$y = w = 33°$ (equal angles subtended by arc SR at the circumference)
$z = 57°$ (angle $OSU = 90°$ since it lies between a tangent and radius and angle $OSP = w$)
Note: Other reasons are possible.

8 There are a variety of ways to prove this.
For example: since M is the midpoint of chord AB, $AM = BM$ and also angle OMA = angle $OMB = 90°$. $OA = OB$, since both are radii. So triangles OAM and OBM are congruent (RHS).

9 **a** 27° (angles subtended by arc DA are equal)
b 54° (angle sum of triangle CDX with vertically opposite angle $CXD = 99°$)
c similar
d 6.87 cm (to 3 s.f.)
e 42.0 cm² (to 3 s.f.)

10 **a** 12 sides
b 114°

11 101°

12 **a** 288 cm²
b 768 cm³

13 Surface area $= 81\pi$ cm²,
volume $= \frac{243}{2}\pi$ cm³

Practise 2.1 – 2.3

1 3

2 1 : 125 000

3 140

4 $\frac{2}{7}$ 28% $\frac{3}{11}$ 0.27

5

	Must be true	Might be true	Cannot be true
$a > b$	✓		
$a \div b = 3$			✓
$a + b > 4$		✓	
$a - b > 4$	✓		

6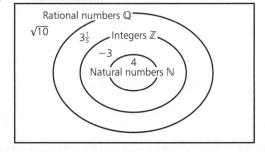
Real numbers $\mathbb{R}$
Rational numbers $\mathbb{Q}$
$\sqrt{10}$
$3\frac{1}{5}$ Integers $\mathbb{Z}$
-3
4
Natural numbers $\mathbb{N}$

7 $4^2 = 16$, so $15 < 4^2$, hence $\sqrt{15} < 4$

     $4^3 = 64$, so $4^3 < 65$, hence $4 < \sqrt[3]{65}$

     $\sqrt{15} < 4 < \sqrt[3]{65}$

8   **a** $3\frac{3}{4} + 2\frac{3}{5} = 5\frac{15 + 12}{20} = 5\frac{27}{20} = 6\frac{7}{20}$

     b $2\frac{5}{6} \div 1\frac{1}{3} = \frac{17}{6} \times \frac{3}{4} = \frac{17}{8} = 2\frac{1}{8}$

9   **a**   2 hours 24 minutes   **b**   3 hours 20 minutes

10   **a**   5.5 km/h   **b**   3 hours 34 minutes

11   **a**   21 seconds   **b** $2\frac{2}{3}$ km

Practise 3.1 – 3.3

1   **a** $6x + 2y$ **b** $7pq + 2p^2$ **c** $5 - 4m$

2   **a**   50   **b**   6

3   162

4 $4x - 12$

5   **a** $4(3x + 1)$ **b** $2v(3u - 1)$

6 $4x + 15y$

7   **a** $p = -0.5$ **b** $q = 4.8$ **c** $t = 3.25$

8 $12 + 1.25x = 20.75$, $x = 7$

9 $a = \dfrac{P - 2b}{2}$

10   **a** $x = -6$ **b** $y = 2.5$ **c** $m = 7$

11   **a**   37

     b $5 - x = y$ transforms to $x = 5 - y$

     c   2

     d $4 - x^2$

Practise 4.1 – 4.4

1   **a**   **i**   60 cm   **ii**   171 cm²

     b   **i**   800 mm   **ii**   23 100 mm²

     c   **i**   25.6 m   **ii**   43.86 m²

2   **a**   **i**   18.8 m (to 1 d.p.)   **ii**   28.3 m² (to 1 d.p.)

     b   **i**   4.8 cm (to 1 d.p.)   **ii**   71.6 cm² (to 1 d.p.)

3   **a**   18 000 mm³   **c**   1 m³

     b   432 cm³   **d**   40 200 cm³ or 0.0402 m³

4   **a**   85.8 cm² (to 1 d.p.)   **b**   192 tiles

5   **a**

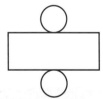

     b   1.81 m² (to 2 d.p.)

     c   177 litres (nearest litre)

6   **a**   **i**   1.69 m² (to 2 d.p.)

         ii   16 900 cm² (nearest 100 cm²)

     b   67 700 cm³ (nearest 100 cm³)

     c   40.6 kg (to 1 d.p.)

7   **a** $\frac{2}{5}$ **b** $\frac{5}{9}$ **c** $\frac{1}{16}$ **d** $\frac{7}{16}$

8

Island	Population	Land area (km²)	Land area per person (m²)
Bermuda	69 000	54	**783**
Malta	408 000	316	**775**
Mauritius	1.3 million	2030	**1562**
Australia	2.2×10^7	7.7×10^6	**350 000**

9   **a**   **i**   Triangular prism   **ii**   366 cm²   **iii**   288 cm³

     b   **i**   Cylinder   **ii**   167 cm²   **iii**   138 cm³

     c   **i**   Cone   **ii**   302 cm²   **iii**   302 cm³

10   **a** $\frac{35}{360} \times 36\pi + \frac{35}{360} \times 16\pi + 2 \times 10 = \frac{91}{18}\pi + 20$

        $= 35.9$ cm (to 1 d.p.)

     b $\frac{35}{360} \times \pi \times 18^2 - \frac{35}{360} \times \pi \times 8^2 = \frac{455}{18}\pi$

        $= 79.4$ cm² (to 1 d.p.)

11   **a** $h = 8$ cm

     b $l = \sqrt{8^2 + 6^2} = 10$ cm;

        surface area $= \pi r l + \pi r^2 = 96\pi$ cm²

12   **a**   Volume of hemisphere : volume of cone

        $= \frac{1}{2} \times \frac{4}{3}\pi r^3 : \frac{1}{3}\pi r^2 h$

        $= \frac{2}{3}\pi r^3 \quad : \frac{1}{3}\pi r^3$ (as $h = r$)

        $= 2 : 1$

     b   Surface area of hemisphere : surface area of cone

        $= \frac{1}{2} \times 4\pi r^2 + \pi r^2 : \pi r l + \pi r^2$

        By Pythagoras, $r^2 + r^2 = l^2$, or $l = \sqrt{2r^2} = r\sqrt{2}$

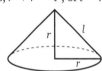

        So ratio $= \frac{1}{2} \times 4\pi r^2 + \pi r^2 : \pi r \times r\sqrt{2} + \pi r^2$

        $= 3\pi r^2 : (1 + \sqrt{2})\pi r^2$

        $= 3 : 1 + \sqrt{2}$

13   **a**   **i**   85 m²   **ii**   2 125 000 litres

     b $2900   **c**   94 hours

14   **a**   314 g (to the nearest g)

     b   6.58 cm (to 2 d.p.)

     c   2.92 cm (to 2 d.p.)

Practise 5.1 – 5.4

1   **a**   **i**   Alert: max. 5 °C, min. −31 °C

         ii   Niagara Falls: max. 21 °C, min. −9 °C

     b   **i**   23 degrees   **ii**   20 degrees

     c   **i**   March   **ii**   June

2   **a**   5   **b** $\frac{1}{3}$ **c**   −8   **d**   −26

3   **a**   582.75 Australian dollars

     b   261.10 Indian rupees

4   52 min 8 s + 30 s (15 pauses) = 52 min 38 s

5   65% of $22 is 30 cents more ($14.30 against $14.00)

6 $6030

7

	Flight 1	Flight 2	Flight 3
Depart A	0836	**1058**	**1918**
Arrive B	**1103**	1325	**2145**
Depart B	**1145**	**1407**	**2227**
Arrive C	**1503**	**1725**	0145

8

Ingredient	Quantity	Price	Unit	Quantity cost
Chicken breasts	500 g	$17.50	1 kg	$8.75
Butter	20 g	$1.45	250 g	$0.12
Honey	15 g	$1.20	330 g	$0.05
Lemon juice	15 ml	$1.45	500 ml	$0.04
Balsamic vinegar	15 ml	$1.20	250 ml	$0.07
TOTAL COST				$9.03

9 **a** $23   **b** $3.45

10 **a** -2 **b** $-\frac{1}{4}$ **c** $-\frac{1}{5}$ **d** $\frac{3}{7}$

11 **a** 65%   **b** 42

12 $749.18

13 **a** 61 074   **b** 34 800

14 **a** $902.49   **b** 4.27% (to 2 d.p.)

15 **a** $340   **b** 4%

Practise 6.1 – 6.2

1 **a** Manfred, by 0.03 m   **b** Thomas, by 0.03 m
  c Manfred, by 0.065 m
  d Manfred. He had higher averages, so he jumped
     further and a smaller range, so was more consistent.
  e Thomas

2 **a** 27 kg   **b** 4.6 kg

3 **a** Adventure   **b** 9 people   **c** 24

4 **a** **i**

Number of bedrooms	Frequency
1	3
2	5
3	7
4	5

ii

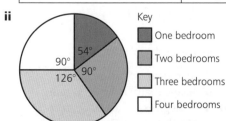

Key
■ One bedroom
■ Two bedrooms
□ Three bedrooms
□ Four bedrooms

b **i**

Price of house, x ($1000s)	Frequency
$60 \leqslant x < 80$	4
$80 \leqslant x < 100$	10
$100 \leqslant x < 120$	2
$120 \leqslant x < 140$	3
$140 \leqslant x < 160$	1

ii

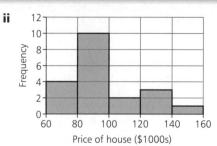

c **i**

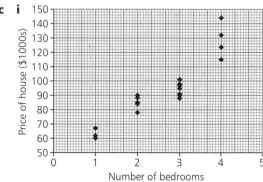

ii It is a positive correlation.

5 **a** 13   **b** **i** 3   **ii** 3   **iii** 4   **iv** 4

6 **a** $10 < x \leqslant 20$

  b $\dfrac{125 + 420 + 300 + 315 + 225 + 44}{80} = \dfrac{1440}{80}$
       $= \$18$

c

Amount spent ($)	0	$\leqslant$10	$\leqslant$20	$\leqslant$30	$\leqslant$40	$\leqslant$50	$\leqslant$60
Cumulative frequency	0	25	53	65	74	79	80

d

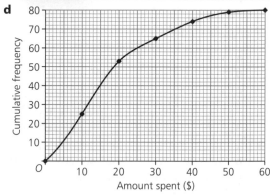

e **i** $15   **ii** $25 - $8 = $17   **iii** 12.5%

7 **a** 1.6

  b $\dfrac{30 + 435 + 1680 + 2640 + 825}{150} = \dfrac{5610}{150} = 37.4$

8 **a** 6.4 km   **b** 8 km   **c** 12%

d **i**

Distance travelled (d km)	Frequency
$0 < d \leqslant 2$	12
$2 < d \leqslant 5$	48
$5 < d \leqslant 7$	60
$7 < d \leqslant 8$	30
$8 < d \leqslant 10$	28
$10 < d \leqslant 14$	22

ii

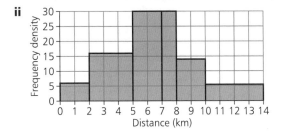

Practise 7.1 – 7.4

Diagrams are drawn half size.

1 a, b i

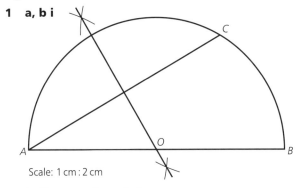

Scale: 1 cm : 2 cm

  b ii It goes through the centre, *O*

2 a, b 1 : 200 000

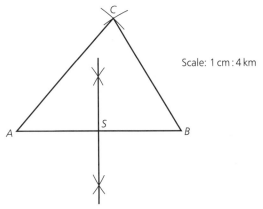

Scale: 1 cm : 4 km

  c 12.0 km

3

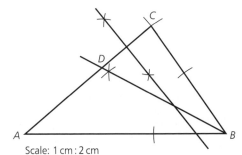

Scale: 1 cm : 2 cm

4 a 1 : 1000

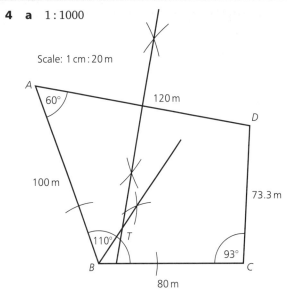

Scale: 1 cm : 20 m

5

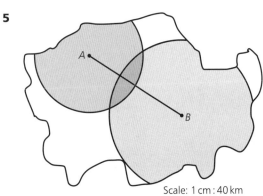

Scale: 1 cm : 40 km

6

Scale: 1 cm : 40 cm

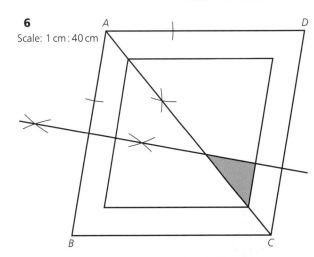

7 a $\begin{pmatrix} 1 \\ 0 \end{pmatrix}$ **b** $\begin{pmatrix} -5 \\ 2 \end{pmatrix}$

  c $\begin{pmatrix} 8 \\ -3 \end{pmatrix}$ **d** $\sqrt{73} = 8.5$ (to 1 d.p.)

8 a i $\overrightarrow{AC} = 2\mathbf{a} + \mathbf{b}$ **ii** $\overrightarrow{DB} = 4\mathbf{a} + 2\mathbf{b}$

  b $\overrightarrow{DB} = 4\mathbf{a} + 2\mathbf{b} = 2(2\mathbf{a} + \mathbf{b}) = 2\overrightarrow{AC}$

    So *DB* and *AC* are parallel, and *ACBD* is a trapezium.

9 a $\begin{pmatrix} 21 & -5 \\ -17 & 3 \\ -6 & 2 \end{pmatrix}$ **b** $\frac{1}{2}\begin{pmatrix} -1 & 1 \\ -5 & 3 \end{pmatrix}$

10 a AB cannot be carried out

b $BC = \begin{pmatrix} -2 & -2 \\ 2 & 3 \end{pmatrix}\begin{pmatrix} 3 & -2 \\ 5 & -3 \end{pmatrix} = \begin{pmatrix} -16 & 10 \\ 21 & -13 \end{pmatrix}$

$$(BC)^{-1} = \frac{1}{(-16 \times -13) - (10 \times 21)}\begin{pmatrix} -13 & -10 \\ -21 & -16 \end{pmatrix}$$

$$= -\frac{1}{2}\begin{pmatrix} -13 & -10 \\ -21 & -16 \end{pmatrix}$$

$$C^{-1} = \frac{1}{(3 \times -3) - (-2 \times 5)}\begin{pmatrix} -3 & 2 \\ -5 & 3 \end{pmatrix} = \begin{pmatrix} -3 & 2 \\ -5 & 3 \end{pmatrix}$$

$$B^{-1} = \frac{1}{(-2 \times 3) - (-2 \times 2)}\begin{pmatrix} 3 & 2 \\ -2 & -2 \end{pmatrix}$$

$$= -\frac{1}{2}\begin{pmatrix} 3 & 2 \\ -2 & -2 \end{pmatrix}$$

$$C^{-1}B^{-1} = \begin{pmatrix} -3 & 2 \\ -5 & 3 \end{pmatrix} - \frac{1}{2}\begin{pmatrix} 3 & 2 \\ -2 & -2 \end{pmatrix}$$

$$= -\frac{1}{2}\begin{pmatrix} -13 & -10 \\ -21 & -16 \end{pmatrix} = (BC)^{-1}$$

11 a $M = \begin{pmatrix} 1 & 1 \\ 2 & -1 \end{pmatrix}$

b $M^{-1} = -\frac{1}{3}\begin{pmatrix} -1 & -1 \\ -2 & 1 \end{pmatrix}$

Practise 8.1 – 8.3

1 a

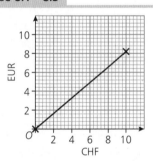

b 3.7 euros

c $4.5 \times 6 = 27$, $3.7 \times 6 = 22.2$ euros or
$27 = 10 + 10 + 7 \rightarrow 8.2 + 8.2 + 5.7 = 22.1$ euros

2 a $60\,\text{km/h}^2$

b The truck is moving at a steady speed of 40 km/h

c $80\,\text{km/h}^2$

d 90 km

3 a $3y = -2x + 12$ **b** $(12, -4)$

4 a

x	-3	-2	-1	0	1	2	3
$2x^2$	18	8	2	0	2	8	18
y	9	0	-5	-6	-3	4	15

b

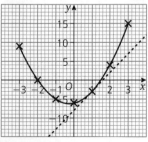

c $x = -2$ and 1.5

d 5

5 a, b

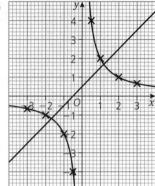

c $x = -1.7$ and 1.2

Practise 9.1 – 9.3

1 a i 3   **ii** 3   **c i** 2   **ii** 2
   b i 0   **ii** 4   **d i** 0   **ii** 3

2 a   **b**

3 a i, ii

Parallelogram

b i, ii Line of symmetry

Kite

iii 50°, 130°, 130°   **iii** 50°, 100°

4

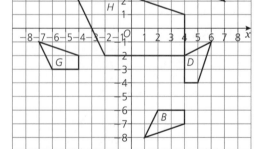

5 a Translation $\begin{pmatrix} -4 \\ 3 \end{pmatrix}$

b Rotation through 90° anticlockwise (or 270° clockwise) about (0, 0)

c Reflection in the y-axis (or $x = 0$)

d Reflection in $y = 4$

e Rotation through 90° clockwise (or 270° anticlockwise) about (0, 0)

f Enlargement, centre $(3, -2)$, scale factor $\frac{1}{4}$

g Enlargement, centre $(6.5, -2)$, scale factor 2

h Translation $\begin{pmatrix} 7 \\ -6.5 \end{pmatrix}$

i Rotation through $90°$ anticlockwise (or $270°$ clockwise) about $(8.5, -3)$

j Reflection in $x = -2.5$

6 a i 7   **ii** 6

  b i 4   **ii** 4

  c i Infinite   **ii** Infinite

7 a i

  b i ii

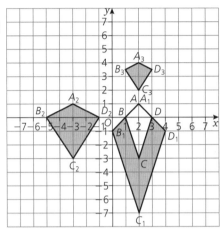

  a ii $1 : 4$

  b iii $2 : 4 : 1$

8 a

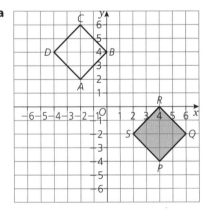

  b i Translation $\begin{pmatrix} 6 \\ -6 \end{pmatrix}$

    ii Rotation of $90°$ anticlockwise (or $270°$ clockwise) about $(4, 4)$

    iii Rotation of $180°$ clockwise (or anticlockwise) about $(1, 1)$ or enlargement with scale factor -1 and centre $(1, 1)$

    iv Rotation of $90°$ clockwise (or $270°$ anticlockwise) about $(-2, -2)$

    v Reflection in $y = x$

9

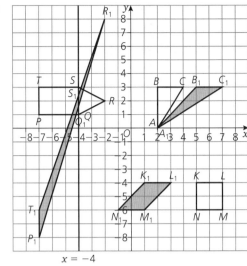

$x = -4$

10 a i Shear with invariant line $y = 2$ and which maps $(3, 3)$ onto $(6, 3)$

    ii Shear with y-axis invariant and which maps $(3, 3)$ onto $(3, 6)$

    Note: Or alternative answers which give the new position of different points.

  b i Enlargement with centre $(-4, 1)$ and scale factor -3

    ii Two-way stretch with horizontal scale factor 2 and invariant line $x = -8$ and vertical scale factor $\frac{1}{2}$ and invariant line $y = 6$

11 a

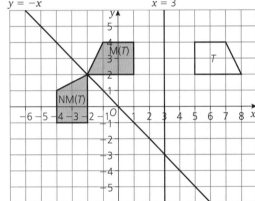

  b Rotation of $90°$ anticlockwise (or $270°$ clockwise) about $(3, -3)$

12

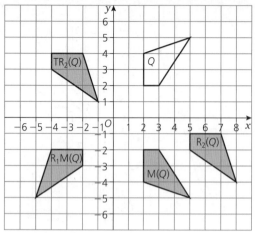

a Reflection in $y = -x$

b Rotation of 90° clockwise (or 270° anticlockwise) about (0, 6)

Practise 10.1 – 10.4

1 **a** $(0.3 + 0.2)^2 \times 400 - \sqrt{4}$ **b** 98 **c** 113.3

2 **a** **i** 7, 13, 19, 25, 31

ii 9, 5, 1, −3, −7

iii 1, 3, 7, 15, 31

b $\frac{1}{2}, \frac{2}{5}, \frac{3}{10}, \frac{4}{17}, \frac{5}{26}$

3 **a** **i** 16 740 000 **ii** 16 737 700

b 23 015 000 ⩽ population < 23 025 000

c 37.5%

4 202 people/km²

5 **a** **i** 1.74×10^4 **ii** 5.328×10^{-3}

b **i** 3 254 000 **ii** 0.00003254

6 **a** **i** −9, −15 **ii** Subtract 6 **iii** $-6n + 21$

b $6n - 3$

c +18

7 **a**

Pattern	1st	2nd	3rd	4th	5th
Lines	3	6	9	12	15
Crosses	4	7	10	13	16

b **i** 21 **ii** 22

c **i** $3n$ **ii** $3n + 1$

d 151

e 75

8

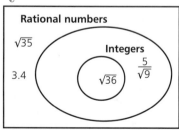

9 **a** $k = 5$ **c** 1155

10 **a** 27.5 km ⩽ distance walked in 1 day < 28.5 km

b Max. = \$499; min. = \$481

11

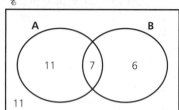

12

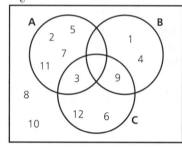

13 **a** 7×10^{-6} **b** $A = 7.5 \times 10^{-3}$

14 **a**

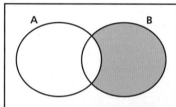

b

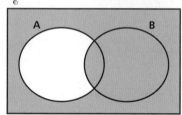

15 **a** $p = 5$ **d** $s = -6$

b $q = 15$ **e** $t = 1\frac{1}{4}$

c $r = -3$

16 **a** **i** 14.5 cm ⩽ height < 15.5 cm

ii 4.325 cm ⩽ radius < 4.375 cm

b 7317 g/cm³ and 6604 g/cm³

c 0.01%

Practise 11.1

1 **a** $\frac{1}{4}$ **b** 0

2 **a** $\frac{12}{25}$ **b** $\frac{17}{25}$ **c** $\frac{4}{5}$

3 **a** $\frac{4}{11}$ **b** 44

4 **a** **i** $\frac{3}{25}$ **ii** $\frac{3}{10}$ **iii** $\frac{7}{10}$

b **i** $\frac{3}{40}$ **ii** $\frac{9}{25}$ **iii** $\frac{16}{25}$

c Mouna's results give better probabilities because she performed the experiment more times

5 **a** $\frac{7}{50}$ **b** 900

6 **a** $\frac{1}{5}$ **b** $\frac{8}{15}$ **c** $\frac{1}{9}$

7 **a**

Travel	Lunch	Outcome	Probability

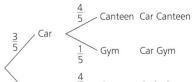

$\frac{4}{5}$ Canteen Car Canteen $\frac{3}{5} \times \frac{4}{5} = \frac{12}{25}$

Car

$\frac{3}{5}$ $\frac{1}{5}$ Gym Car Gym $\frac{3}{5} \times \frac{1}{5} = \frac{3}{25}$

$\frac{4}{5}$ Canteen Cycle Canteen $\frac{2}{5} \times \frac{4}{5} = \frac{8}{25}$

$\frac{2}{5}$ Cycle

$\frac{1}{5}$ Gym Cycle Gym $\frac{2}{5} \times \frac{1}{5} = \frac{2}{25}$

b **i** P(cycle and canteen) $= \frac{8}{25}$

   ii P(cycle or gym or both)

   $= 1 - \text{P(car and canteen)} = 1 - \frac{12}{25} = \frac{13}{25}$

Practise 12.1 – 12.3

1 $r = \sqrt{\dfrac{V}{\pi h}}$

2 **a** $x \geqslant 6$ **b** $y > -1$

3 $(1.5, -1)$

4 $y \geqslant -2, y < x + 2, y \leqslant 8 - 2x$

5 **a** $x + y \leqslant 14$ **c** $x \leqslant 8$

b $x + y \geqslant 9$ **d** $x \geqslant \frac{1}{2}y$ or $y \leqslant 2x$

e

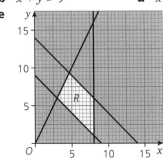

6 **a** $p^2 - 64$ **b** $4q^2 + 5q - 6$

7 **a** $(m + 1)(m + 7)$ **c** $(t + 1)(5t - 2)$

b $(n + 2)(n - 3)$ **d** $(p + 5)(q - 2)$

8 **a** $3(x + 1)(x - 1)$ **b** $2(y - 3)^2$

9 **a** $\dfrac{11}{10x}$ **b** $\dfrac{(y - 1)}{(2y + 1)}$

10 **a** $x = -5$ or 1.5 **c** $m = -0.64$ or 0.39

b $a = 9, b = 83$

Practise 13.1 – 13.2

1 $65.9°$ (to 1 d.p.)

2 $109.5°$ (to 1 d.p.)

3 **a** $36.9°$ (to 1 d.p.)   **b** $10.7\,\text{m}$ (to 1 d.p.)

4 **a** $9.3\,\text{cm}$ (to 1 d.p.)   **b** $65.3°$ (to 1 d.p.)

5 **a** $78°$ **c** $124.0°$ (to 1 d.p.)

b $15.3\,\text{km}$ (to 1 d.p.)

6 **a** $249.4\,\text{cm}^2$ (to 1 d.p.)

b **i** $10.4\,\text{cm}$ (to 1 d.p.)

   ii $54.7°$ (to 1 d.p.)

Glossary

2-way table a table used to show two different pieces of information.

A

acceleration the rate at which speed changes with time.

acute less than 90°.

acute-angled triangle a triangle with all of the angles less than 90°.

adjacent side the side adjacent to the known or required angle in a right-angled triangle.

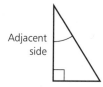

Adjacent side

alternate angles angles formed on opposite sides of a transversal between parallel lines.

ambiguous case something that can have two different possible answers.

analogue showing a reading with a moving hand on a dial (opposite of **digital**).

angle a turn or change in direction.

angle bearings angles measured clockwise from North to describe a direction.

angle bisector a line that cuts an angle in half.

angle of depression looking down, the angle between the horizontal and the line of sight.

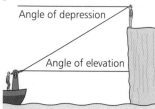

Angle of depression

Angle of elevation

angle of elevation looking up, the angle between the line of sight and the horizontal.

annual salary amount of money a person is paid per year.

appreciate increase in value.

appreciation the increase in value of an item.

arc part of the circumference of a circle.

Minor arc

Major arc

area the amount of space inside a 2-D shape.

average speed the ratio of distance ÷ time.

axes (singular: **axis**) fixed reference lines for the measurement of coordinates.

B

bar chart a chart for displaying data, using parallel bars or columns of the same width.

base number the number which is being raised to a power.

biased of an outcome that is distorted and not as expected.

BIDMAS order in which operations are performed: **B**rackets, **I**ndices (powers: squares, cubes, …), **D**ivision, **M**ultiplication, **A**ddition, **S**ubtraction.

bisect cut in half.

bonus an extra payment.

boundary edge of an area on a graph.

C

capacity the amount a container holds when it is full.

Cartesian coordinates two axes at right angles.

centre of enlargement the lines joining corresponding points on an object and its image all meet at the centre of enlargement.

centre of rotation fixed point at the centre of a rotation.

certain having a probability of 1.

changing the subject changing which letter is on the left-hand side of a formula.

chord a straight line joining two points on the circumference of a circle.

circle the locus of a point moving at a given distance from a fixed point.

circumference the distance around the outside (perimeter) of a circle.

class boundaries the greatest and smallest values in a class.

coefficient the number in front of a quantity such as *x*.

collinear lying on a straight line.

common factor a factor that is common to two or more numbers or terms.

common multiple a multiple that is common to two or more numbers.

complement the complement of set **A** is everything outside set **A**.

composite function two functions combined.

composite shape a shape made from simple shapes.

compound interest interest which is added to the principal.

congruent having exactly the same size and shape.

consecutive next to each other.

constant of proportionality the constant value of the ratio between two proportional quantities.

continuous data data that can have any value within a range.

conversion factor a number used to convert from one unit of measurement to another.

conversion graph a graph used to convert from one unit of measurement to another.

convert change one unit of measurement to another.

correlation a connection between two sets of data.

corresponding angles angles formed on the same sides of a transversal between parallel lines.

cosine the ratio of the adjacent side to the hypotenuse.

cosine rule a rule connecting sides and angles of a non-right-angled triangle. $a^2 = b^2 + c^2 - 2bc \cos A$.

cost price the original price of an item you are selling.

cross-section a face formed by cutting through an object at right angles.

cube a 3-D solid consisting of six square faces.

cube number the number you get when you multiply three lots of the number together.

cube root opposite of cubing a number.

cubic function a function that contains a term in x^3.

cuboid a 3-D solid consisting of six rectangular faces.

currency the unit of money that is used in a country. Different countries use different currencies.

cyclic quadrilateral a quadrilateral whose vertices lie on the circumference of a circle.

cylinder a 3-D solid with a circle as its cross-section.

deceleration the rate at which speed decreases with time.

decrease go down in value.

degree unit of measurement for angles.

denominator the number on the bottom of a fraction.

deposit money paid to start with.

depreciate decrease in value.

depreciation the decrease in value of an item.

determinant a value computed using the elements of a square matrix.

diameter the distance from one point on the circumference to another point passing through the centre.

Diameter

difference the difference between successive terms of a linear sequence.

digital showing a reading as numbers on a display (opposite of **analogue**).

direct proportion two quantities such that as one increases so does the other by the same ratio.

direct variation same as direct proportion.

directed number a positive or negative number or zero.

direction the direction of a vector.

discontinuous having a break.

discount an amount taken off the selling price of an item.

discrete data data that can have only certain values within a range.

double time hourly rate of pay that is twice the normal hourly rate.

 E

edge the line where two faces of a solid meet.

element a member of a set.

empty set see **null set**.

enlargement a transformation in which the shape of an object stays the same, but its size usually changes.

equally likely outcomes outcomes that have the same probability.

equidistant at the same distance.

equivalent fractions fractions that are equal in value.

event a set of outcomes in probability.

expand multiply all the terms inside brackets by the term outside the brackets (opposite of **factorise**).

experimental probability the ratio of the number of times the event occurs to the total number of trials.

exponential having a constant base raised to a variable power.

expression a series of terms connected by addition and subtraction signs.

exterior angle the angle you turn through at each vertex when going round the perimeter of a polygon.

 F

face the surface of a solid which is enclosed by edges.

factor a whole number which divides exactly into another whole number.

factorise take a common factors outside a set of brackets (opposite of **expand**).

fair unbiased.

formula (plural: **formulae**) rule expressed in words or letters.

frequency the number of times a value occurs in a set of data.

function a rule which changes one number into another number.

 G

gradient a measure of how steep a line is.

grouping putting data into groups.

GST (General Sales Tax) tax added to the selling price of something.

H

highest common factor (HCF) the largest factor which is common to two or more numbers.

hire purchase way of buying items and paying for them over a number of months.

histogram a chart that displays the frequency of data by the areas of bars.

horizontal at right angles to the vertical.

hourly rate of pay rate of pay for each hour worked.

hypotenuse the longest side of a right-angled triangle. It is always opposite the right angle.

 I

identity matrix the matrix, **I**, that does not produce any change when multiplied with another matrix.

image the new shape after a transformation.

impossible having a probability of 0.

improper fraction a fraction in which the numerator is larger than the denominator.

included angle the angle between two given sides.

income tax tax paid on the money you earn.

increase go up in value.

index power of a number.

index form (index notation) a way of writing a number using powers.

inequality a statement about the relative size or order of two objects using $<$, $\leq$, $>$ and $\geq$.

inequation a statement similar to an equation but using $<$, $\leq$, $>$ or $\geq$ instead of $=$.

infinite continuing for ever.

instalments equal regular payments.

integers $\ldots, -5, -4, -3, -2, -1, 0, 1, 2, 3, 4, 5, \ldots$

intercept where a line crosses the y-axis.

interest the charge for borrowing or lending money.

interior angle the angle inside a polygon.

interquartile range the difference between the upper and lower quartiles.

intersection
1. a point where two graphs meet.
2. a set that is made up of all the elements that belong to both of two different sets.

invariant line a line on which points in a one-way stretch or a shear do not move.

inverse something that is reversed in order or effect.

inverse matrix a matrix M^{-1} such that $M \times M^{-1} =$ the identity matrix.

inverse proportion a relation between two variables, in which one variable increases as the other decreases.

irrational number a number that cannot be written as a fraction.

least common multiple (LCM) the lowest multiple that is common to two or more numbers.

like terms terms containing the same variables raised to the same power, which can be combined by adding or subtracting.

line of best fit a straight line that goes between points on a graph, passing as close as possible to all of them.

line of symmetry the fold line when a 2-D shape can be folded so that one half fits exactly over the other.

line segment the part of a line joining two points.

line symmetry symmetry in which a 2-D shape divides a shape into two congruent halves which are mirror images of each other.

linear equation an equation that does not contain any powers or roots of x or y such as x^2 or $\sqrt{y}$.

linear sequence a sequence in which the difference between consecutive terms is the same for all terms.

line a one-dimensional figure extending infinitely in both directions.

locus (plural: **loci**) the path followed by a moving point.

loss if you sell something for less than you paid for it, you make a loss.

lower bound the smallest possible value of a rounded quantity.

lower quartile the value one quarter of the way from the lowest value.

lowest common denominator the lowest common multiple of the denominators of two or more fractions.

magnitude the size of a vector.

mapping the process which changes one number into another number.

matrix (plural: **matrices**) a rectangular set of numbers.

mean a way of calculating how much each value would be if all the values were shared equally.

measure of dispersion a measure of how spread out data are.

median the middle value, when data are put in order.

membership all the elements in a set.

mirror line a **line of symmetry**.

mixed number a fractions that consists of a whole number part and a fractional part.

modal of the score or class with the highest frequency.

modal class the class with the highest frequency.

mode the score with the highest frequency.

multiple the product of an integer with another integer.

multiplier method multiplying a quantity by a fraction representing a ratio.

mutually exclusive having no outcome in common.

natural numbers the counting numbers, 1, 2, 3, 4, 5, …

negative correlation a correlation in which one quantity increases as the other decreases.

negative integer any negative whole number.

net a 2-D pattern that can be cut out and folded to form a 3-D shape.

no correlation the points on a graph do not appear to follow a trend.

non-terminating decimal a decimal that does not end.

nth term counting from the 1st term in a sequence, the term in position n.

null set a set that contains no elements.

numerator the number on top of a fraction.

object the original shape before a transformation.

obtuse greater than 90° but less than 180°.

obtuse-angled triangle a triangle with one of the angles more than 90°.

odometer an instrument that measures the distance a car has travelled.

operations $+$, $-$, $\times$, $\div$.

opposite side the side opposite to the known or required angle in a right-angled triangle.

Opposite side

order of rotational symmetry the number of different positions in which a shape looks the same during a complete turn.

ordered pair a pair that go together in order, like coordinates.

origin the point (0, 0) where graph axes cross, where both coordinates are zero.

outcome result.

overtime extra hours worked.

parallel parallel lines are the same distance apart everywhere along their length.

per annum every year.

percentile in a set of data, the value at a given percentage of the way from the lowest value.

perimeter the total distance around the sides of a shape.

perpendicular at right angles (90°).

perpendicular bisector a line that cuts a line in half at right angles.

pictogram a way of representing data using pictures and a key.

pie chart a circular chart showing frequencies as proportions.

plane of symmetry a plane that divides a 3-D solid into two congruent halves which are mirror images of each other.

point the intersection of two lines.

polygon a two-dimensional shape with straight sides.

position vector a vector from the origin (0, 0) to a point.

position-to-term rule a rule for a sequence linking the term number to the value of that term.

positive correlation as one quantity increases, the other increases.

positive integer any positive whole number.

possibility diagram a diagram in which dots represent possible events.

power the number of times a base number is multiplied.

pre-multiplying putting a transformation matrix at the front.

prime number a number that has exactly two factors.

principal the amount of money invested.

prism a 3-D solid whose cross-section is the same throughout its length.

probability scale a scale on which probabilities are shown.

profit if you sell something for more than you paid for it, you make a profit.

proper subset the same as a **subset** but where **B** contains additional elements not in **A**. A proper subset is written $A \subset B$.

proportion comparing one part to the total amount.

Q

quadratic function a function in which x^2 is the highest power of x.

qualitative descriptive but not numerical.

quantitative numerical.

R

radius (plural: **radii**) the distance from one point on the circumference to the centre.

range the difference between the largest item and the smallest item in a set of data.

rate the rate of interest per year for borrowing or lending money.

rate of change the ratio of a change in one variable to a change in another variable.

ratio comparing two or more quantities with each other.

rational number any number that can be written in the form $\frac{p}{q}$, where p and q are integers.

raw data data as collected, before being processed.

real number any rational or irrational number.

reciprocal a fraction turned upside down.

reciprocal function a graph involving a reciprocal such as $y = \frac{1}{x}$.

recurring decimal a decimal with an infinite number of decimal places, in which the last digit or group of digits are repeated.

reflection a transformation that gives an image which looks like the reflection of the object in a mirror.

reflex greater than 180° but less than 360°.

region an area on a graph.

regular having all sides equal and all angles equal.

relative frequency
$$\frac{\text{the number of outcomes for the event}}{\text{total number of trials}}.$$

reverse percentage working back from a percentage to find the original quantity.

right angle an angle of 90°.

right-angled triangle a triangle with one of the angles 90°.

rotation turning an object through a given angle about a fixed point.

rotational symmetry looking exactly the same after a rotation of less than 360°.

rounding replacing a number with one that is approximately equal.

rule a general statement.

S

sample space diagram a table showing all the possible outcomes.

scalar a single number.

scale drawing accurate drawing that shows the exact shape but does not use the actual size.

scale factor a number that tells you how many times bigger the object is than the image.

scatter diagram a diagram that that shows two sets of data as points on a graph.

sector an area of a circle cut off by two radii and an arc.

segment an area of a circle cut off by a chord and an arc.

self-inverse being its own inverse.

selling price the price you sell something for.

semicircle half a circle.

sequence a set of numbers or patterns with a given rule or pattern.

set a collection of objects or numbers, usually having something in common.

shear a transformation in which points move in a direction parallel to the invariant line.

significant figures the digits of a number, starting from the first non-zero digit.

similar having the same shape, but being different in size.

simple interest the charge for borrowing or lending money. $I = \frac{PRT}{100}$.

simplest form the form with the smallest possible whole numbers in the numerator and the denominator of a fraction, or the smallest possible whole numbers in a ratio.

simplifying collecting the like terms.

simultaneous equations two equations with two unknowns.

sine the ratio of the opposite side to the hypotenuse.

sine rule a rule connecting sides and angles of a non-right-angled triangle.
$$\frac{a}{\sin A} = \frac{b}{\sin B} = \frac{c}{\sin C}.$$

solid a three-dimensional shape.

solve work out.

square number the result of multiplying an integer by itself.

square root opposite of squaring a number.

standard form a way of writing very large and very small numbers using a number between 1 and 10 multiplied by a power of 10.

stretch transformation in which points move in a direction perpendicular to the invariant line.

strong correlation a correlation in which the points on a graph are very close to a line of best fit.

subset if every element of **A** is also in **B**, then **A** is a subset of **B** written **A ⊆ B**.

substitution replacing the letters in an expression with numbers to find its value.

surface area the total area of the faces of a solid.

tally charts a method of showing a set of data.

tangent
1. A straight line that touches a curve at only one point.
2. The ratio of the opposite side to the adjacent side in a right-angled triangle.

term an expression forming part of a sequence, or an equation.

terminating decimal a decimal with a finite number of decimal places.

term-to-term rule a rule for a sequence linking one term to the value of the next term.

time-and-a-half an hourly rate of one-and-a-half times the normal hourly rate.

transformation a change of the position or the size of a shape.

transforming changing the subject of a formula.

translation a transformation in which the object moves across the page, but is not rotated or reflected.

transversal a line that cuts two or more parallel lines.

tree diagram a tree-shaped diagram that shows all the outcomes for each event, and the probabilities.

trial an experiment that is repeated a large number of times.

trigonometry the study of right-angled triangles.

union a set that is made up of all the elements of two or more sets.

unit vector a vector that is one unit long.

unitary method finding the value of one unit of a quantity.

unitary ratio any ratio in the form $1 : n$.

Universal Set the set containing all elements to be considered.

unknown a value you are trying to find.

unlike terms terms containing different variables which can be combined by adding or subtracting.

upper bound the smallest possible value that is greater than the value of a rounded quantity.

upper quartile the value three-quarter of the way from the lowest value.

variable a quantity that can take different values.

VAT (Value Added Tax) tax added to the selling price of something.

vector way of writing a change of position in two directions.

Venn diagram a way of showing the elements of sets in a diagram.

vertex (plural: **vertices**) a point where three or more edges of a solid meet.

vertical a line at right angles to the horizontal.

volume the amount of space inside a 3-D shape.

weak correlation a correlation in which the points on a graph are not close to a line of best fit.

weekly wage the amount of money a person is paid per week.

x-coordinate the first number in a pair of coordinates to identify the position of a point on a graph.

y-coordinate the second number in a pair of coordinates to identify the position of a point on a graph.

zero matrix the matrix which does not produce any change when added to or subtracted from another matrix.